# Limp Bizkit

## Colin Devenish

 St. Martin's Griffin ≈ New York

www.stmartins.com

Design by Heidi L. Eriksen

Library of Congress Cataloging-in-Publication Data

Devenish, Colin.
    Limp Bizkit / Colin Devenish.—1st. ed.
        p.   cm.
    ISBN 0-312-26349-X
    1. Limp Bizkit (Musical group) 2. Rock musicians—United States—Biography. I. Title.

ML421.L55 D48 2000
782.42166'092'2—dc21
[B]
                                                    00-039061


First Edition: October 2000

10   9   8   7   6   5   4   3   2   1

Mad Props, Big Ups, and Much Love
to Ma, Pa, and Al, RM, Spoon, Am Night, Ed Leon,
Brandes, Giles, Boris, and Fatty

# One

The summer of 1990 was a bad time to be Fred Durst. Back home in Jacksonville, Florida, after a stint in the navy, a failed marriage, and fathering a baby daughter, Durst had no real prospects of his own, and there were few people who would have wanted to step into his shell-toed shoes. Needing a job, Fred turned to his father Bill, a retired cop who had recently begun a landscaping business, for employment. Fred lived with his father in Jacksonville while his mother Anita and his brother Corey stayed in his hometown of Gastonia, N.C., so Corey could finish high school. Summer temperatures in Jacksonville hover in the low 90s, with humidity at a sweltering 80 percent. For Fred, working as a foreman for Cloverleaf Pro Landscape in Jacksonville's merciless summer sun could not have seemed farther from the Hollywood Hills he would one day call home.

"I was a foreman at a landscape company, cutting grass in hot-ass Florida. Then I started working part-time at this surf shop. Then I learned to tattoo, and I started doing it part-time just for fun," Durst said in a 1999 interview with allmusic.com. "I fucked a few people up before I was good. Then I started getting really good at tattooing, so I just kept doing it because I was making so much money."

Making the cover of *Rolling Stone* and mugging for MTV couldn't have been further from inking tatts and cutting grass as Durst was in the early 90s, but even as he manned a mower up one green swath of lawn and down the next, an idea for a band had formed in his head—a band that inside of a decade would top the charts and spend more time on MTV than Carson Daly. Even the most optimistic fortune-teller could not have foreseen that this small town kid who grew up break-dancing in Gastonia, N.C. would trade power mowers for power brokers and skateboarding for *Billboard*ing at No. 1.

Fred was born in Jacksonville but grew up in Gastonia, after his parents returned to the city where his mother had been born when he was one and a half years old. Although Fred and younger brother Corey grew up doing normal kid stuff, like playing Little League and getting into school yard scraps, Fred later said he always felt like an outsider, like the kid in *Sesame Street* who does his own thing. "I got my feelings hurt a lot. I was the quiet one—always wanted to be the leader of the team, never got picked, you know," Fred told the *Washington Post*. "Not a sob story—just, like, that kid."

Being different was fun sometimes, like when Fred dressed up as a member of Kiss for Halloween in the third grade. Beaming in black tights, with a silver foil codpiece and knee pads in front of the Durst family fireplace and 70s-style wood-paneled walls, Fred looks every bit the triumphant outsider in a picture taken of the event.

Fred Durst grew up fighting in Gastonia, getting repeatedly pummeled for liking a kind of music that challenged people's conceptions of what music is. By his own admission Fred didn't win any of the fights but he did learn a resiliency and determination that would one day help him and his bandmates in Limp Bizkit battle their way to the top of the heap. "I remember the first fight I got in. I was in sixth grade, and some kid got me in a headlock and I couldn't get out," Fred said to *Request* magazine. "He thought he had won, but I went up to him when he was at baseball practice a couple weeks later, and I picked up a baseball bat and cracked him right in the knees."

That punch-counterpunch philosophy would later help Fred take detractors' comments and turn them around. When women stayed away from Limp Bizkit shows in droves, Fred came up with the idea for the "Ladies Night in Cambodia" tour.

With their male fan base cemented, the band offered free tickets to the first three hundred women in attendance each night. Within a couple years there were as many, if not more, women and girls at the barricades outside the MTV studios screaming for the band, as men.

Located within two hours of the foothills of the Great Smokey Mountains and four hours from the pristine beaches of North and South Carolina, the beauty of the great outdoors was readily accessible to young Fred, but what interested him and eventually became his calling was happening hundreds of miles to the north, in the urban playgrounds and parks of New York City. Part of the first generation to grow up listening to rap, Fred's friends in Gastonia were both black and white kids, and both helped shape his musical tastes. "I've been listening to hip-hop since I was twelve. I grew up in North Carolina, and my friends were black, and I was listening to Michael Jackson and Donna Summer and Led Zeppelin—it didn't matter," Durst told the Addicted To Noise web site. "When hip-hop came out to the world in the 80s, I was feelin' it, and then I just became a part of it—bustin' rhymes, break-dancing and everything when I was like twelve or thirteen years old."

In Gastonia, a rural burg of 50,000, music tastes adhered closely to color lines. Fred's enjoyment of a variety of styles aggravated his culturally less advanced peers who thought the rock stars on your favorite records should share your skin color. "There was a jock scene and a bad-boy redneck scene and a black scene. I was part of them all in a weird way," Fred said to *Rolling Stone*. "Until the Beastie Boys came out, I was called 'nigger lover.' I mean I couldn't go to parties, I would get ganged by so many fuckin' people. I learned how to fight good."

Fred's view of himself as an outsider became more pronounced in high school. If it wasn't listening to the wrong kind of music, it was talking to the wrong girl at the wrong time. Either way, Fred began to see himself as a victim, a point of view that would later carry over to his music. "I once went to a party with this girl, and her ex-boyfriend was there," Fred remembered in *Request*. "So, I go into the kitchen to get a drink, and all of a sudden I'm cornered by ten guys. They were all pounding on me. I got loose and escaped and they chased me through the neighborhood. I had to climb up on a roof and hide there. That kind of thing sticks with you forever."

Melissa Barnhill of Spartanburg, S.C., hung out with Fred when he was counting the days until graduation from Hunter Huss High, and told the *Charlotte Observer* that Fred didn't seem to be much of a loner and had his own scene with the skate punks that she admired. "He was just a little skate rat and ran around with other skaters who were into a bunch of different kinds of music. I thought they were really cool because they dressed different. They weren't like everybody else. That's why he might have thought he was an outcast."

The years Fred spent at Hunter Huss High School in Gastonia by his own admission were not spent with his nose stuffed in a book and he was just happy to walk away with a diploma. "I was definitely not a good student in school. I was the teacher's favorite dude, I passed cuz I was, like, kissing my teacher's ass and pretty much I never did my homework," Fred explained in an interview on *Modern Rock Live*. "I don't even know how I made it. It was like a social event for me. . . . I did graduate because they couldn't stand me . . . but that's it."

Fred got into his share of scrapes growing up but his wild side was kept in check in part by seeing the things that happened to his dad in the course of his duties as an undercover narcotics officer for the Gastonia police. "I've seen him come home shot when I was real young, and I've seen the people he had to deal with because of drugs and stuff, and that kept me out of it. He's been shot a couple of times, and he'd come home from the hospital, and you're just like, 'Holy shit!' There were crazy raids and shit. The drug dealers attacked him. It was just crazy shit. I remember when pot came into my life, but I never did anything else. I was too scared to."

By raising Fred in the Lutheran faith, Bill and Anita hoped to give young Fred the same values they'd grown up with and a different viewpoint from the pop culture he so readily embraced. Anita explained the importance of religion in the Durst household in an interview with the *NME*. "I've raised Fred with very strong faith in our family, and Fred is very very serious about his faith. He prays every day and he thanks God for what He's given him. That's the way I raised him and that's what makes me the most proud. I don't think God gives you things because you pray, I think God takes *care* of you because you pray . . ."

When not attending the family's Lutheran church, Fred worshipped at the temple of hip-hop and not just the New York rap that had trickled its way down south. In the same way that the Treacherous Three or the Cold Crush Brothers spun Fred's head right round, hearing Black Sabbath's sludgy riffs made him sit up and take notice of a sound coming from the opposite side of the spectrum. "Back in the day, my cousin had the album opened up and I was like, 'damn, this guy's voice is awesome.' I saw that video, 'Paranoid,' you know, and Ozzy's hair was all in his face, and he was just singing," Fred told MTV. "I think we all like Ozzy Osbourne, I mean, you can't help but like Ozzy Osbourne; his voice, his melody, his music, his everything is great."

Bill and Anita Durst both worked, Bill as a cop and Anita at a mental health hospital and Fred describes his upbringing as middle-class with all the basics covered. Like many parents, Fred told all-music.com that his insistence on having just the right kind of kicks and clothes, when cheaper quality alternatives existed puzzled them. "It was cool. Probably $50,000 a year, family income. For the 70s and 80s, that was pretty normal. It was nothing special. No name-brand shit. We had to be wearing these shitty shoes. They didn't understand why you had to pay fifty bucks for a pair of Nikes when you could have Kugas for five bucks. That kind of old-fashioned thinking was going on."

While Fred's parents weren't exactly eager to spring for his fashion favorites, they tended to roll with the punches as he grew up and didn't give him flak even when it wasn't exactly clear where he was headed. "Earrings, rap music, punk rock, and crazy clothes, and a crazy variety of friends was definitely not a happening thing for them. But they took it as it went," Fred said to allmusic.com.

Even though Gastonia couldn't have been farther from the urban landscape where rap was beginning to evolve into the style of music that would dominate the charts in the late 90s, the friendships Fred made at a young age gave him a peek at where the music was going. "I had a lot of black friends, and all their relatives lived in New York, so they had all the stuff from New York right there in the 80s, right when hip-hop started coming out," Fred told allmusic.com. "For break-dancing and skateboarding and everything, it was just the right place to be. I had a couple friends who were into what I was into: break-dancing, rapping, deejaying, skate-boarding."

Honing his style included listening to the best emcees at the time and studying their flow and picking up ideas from them. Just as a young guitarist drives his family crazy with his first clumsy runs through "Stairway to Heaven," Fred wore the grooves off his favorite rap records and practiced rapping like his hero Rakim whenever he got the chance. "The way he rhymed and would go into mind trips and move the crowd and just go crazy yet still is so monotone," Fred recalled in the Q&A released with Limp Bizkit's first record. "He had so much power, I went and saw them in concert and I was like, 'Oh my gosh, man.' This guy Rakim is insane. He moved me so much, I used to listen to them nonstop."

As Fred became more versed in hip-hop culture, rapping in front of the mirror and break-dancing on the kitchen floor didn't cut it anymore. Wanting to show off his mad skills, he sought out competitions and public venues to show his stuff. "When I was young, I'd go to hip-hop contests, and I just did it," Fred told allmusic.com. "I was doing talent shows and break-dancing contests at the mall against people—just crews battling and rapping with a beat-boxer. Then I actually got turntables and a mixer in '85 and started to learn how to deejay."

While Fred was wearing out the soles of his Kugas perfecting his break-dancing moves, Wes Borland, a couple states away in Nashville, Tennessee, was banging his head to the sounds of Metallica, Anthrax, and Testament and nodding along to the punk rantings of the Circle Jerks and Minor Threat. Nashville is known for being home to the Grand Ole Opry and wearing its love of country on its rolled up flannel sleeve, but the music scene there failed to capture the imagination of young Wes Borland. Wes's musical heroes in junior high and high school wouldn't have been caught dead in cowboy boots let alone singing about lost women, sick horses, and regrettable decisions made after too much whiskey. "My father plays acoustic folk music. I got my first guitar when I was twelve. I grew up in Nashville, [but] I didn't want an acoustic. I was completely anticountry!" Wes told *Maximum Guitar*.

Wes initially expressed an interest in playing drums—putting the pots and pans in the kitchen through the paces—but when the idea of his percussive practice in the Borland home failed to appeal to his parents, he settled on the guitar and began taking lessons from a member of their church. Wes recalled for *Maximum Guitar*, "I would bring in something, and my teacher would go, 'I've never heard of the Damned. Don't you want to play some Merle Haggard?' "

Wes didn't have to go any farther than down

the hall to find his first bass player, as his younger brother Scott soon picked up a four string and began thunking out bass lines to accompany Wes's noodlings on the guitar. At an age when most siblings spend all their free time finding new and innovative ways to torture each other, Wes and his younger brother Scott put their creative energies toward music. "Up to this day, my brother is one of my best friends in the world," Wes told *Guitar One*. "For him picking up a bass for the first time, and me picking up a guitar and having something that we could do together—something that we could actually help each other get good at, and that we could do together—was just awesome."

Life at home meant Wes showed his face at his father's Presbyterian church a little more often than he might have liked and had to toe the line as long as he lived under the same roof as his parents. "I was baptized and pretty much made to go to church every day of my younger life," Wes said to launch.com. "That was pretty much the rule. If I was living in [my parents' house] I had to go to church. That ended when I was about eighteen, after I moved out. I'm not a real big fan of organized religion. . . . Growing up in the home I did, I had a fine childhood—there was nothing wrong with it, but I'm searching for other truths right now."

Even though Wes felt confined by the hours he logged in unwilling worship, he told *Guitar World* that his parents encouraged him to have an open mind, even when his interests were sometimes at odds with their beliefs. "No matter what I got into, both my parents were really involved; they always knew what I was doing. I remember in junior high, some kid had a copy of this occult book called *The Necronomicon*, which at that age was a really evil, exciting, weird thing to know about. . . . So I went home and said, 'I want to get this book.' And my dad went, 'Okay, let's go get it.' We went to the book store and we got it, this horrible, evil thing, with a pentagram on the front. He said, 'When you're done with it, let me have a look at it.' "

Growing up the son of a Presbyterian minister might not seem like a gateway to life as a rock star, but Wes credits his father with encouraging his interests, even when it involved putting himself in situations that would make most God-fearing Christians cringe. "When I said I wanted to go see Judas Priest and Megadeth and Testament, he took me to the concert," said Wes in *Guitar World*. "He said he had a great time, and laughed about somebody passing a joint to him."

Wes attended Hillsboro High School, in the southern section of Nashville. Even with a student-body population hovering around 1,300 students Wes, like Fred, felt the freak during the so-called best years of his life, spending his time on campus wishing that his tormentors would magically stop breathing. "It was horrible. I got picked on and beat up every single day. I secretly wished in the back of my mind that those people would die. I prayed for the courage to fight back, you know? But I never wanted to kill them. With guns. That's extremely wrong, you know?" Wes explained to *Guitar World*, qualifying his remarks in the wake of the shooting deaths at Columbine High School in Colorado.

In a day and age when kids spend more time watching TV than they do with their parents, the support the members of Limp Bizkit received growing up seems like something straight out of an episode of *Leave It to Beaver*. "Fred's mom is fantastic. She's this hilarious lady, and she actually works at a church as an office administrator. John and Sam, their parents are still married and together," Wes said to *Guitar*. "Lethal's parents are wonderful. We all have really good parents. We're all still really close with all our parents, and they've all been super-supportive."

Having slummed his way through high school, Fred evaluated his prospects upon graduation and decided a stint in the navy might be just the thing to get his life going. He was eighteen with no job skills and no real desire to begin a career in the bustling metropolis of Gastonia. As Fred told *Rolling Stone*, the time before he agreed to get a buzz cut and spend grueling weeks under the direction of crabby drill sergeants was a real low point. "I was such a fuckin' loser. I thought, 'My dad can't stand me, man. I'm gonna fuckin' go in the navy and he'll be proud of me then.' "

Shipped out to California, Fred spent eighteen months in the navy, doing nearly all the things a parent wouldn't want their son to do, namely, fathering a daughter at a young age and spending time in jail after a scuffle with his ex-wife and her lover, before ultimately getting an honorable discharge from the navy after a skating accident.

As Fred explained it to Alex Green of homegrown.net, his involvement with music helped steer his volatile temper toward more productive ends. "When we started writing music I would live with it and every song would make me think of someone else who fucked me over, or something else I learned from something, and I realized I could bring it out in my music instead of being a violent person. I've been in jail before for being a violent person. I'm fucked up in the head a little bit."

After originally moving back to North Carolina to work at the Rolling Thunder skate park, Fred decided to join his dad in Jacksonville and begin his assault on the First Coast's lawns and gardens. Mike Geiger, owner of Agony, a Jacksonville tattoo studio, lived with Fred from mid-1991 to the summer of 1992 in the Meadowood Apartments out on Fort Caroline Road in the Arlington neighborhood of Jacksonville. Having met through the cousin of a friend, Geiger said he and Fred passed the time skating and sketching and it was during this time that Fred began giving tattoos professionally with Geiger at East Coast Tattoos. Geiger remembered a favorite skating haunt that he and Fred used to hit up in their free time. "He was okay, he wouldn't get sponsored but he wouldn't get made fun of either. We used to skate at Kona here in Jacksonville, at a concrete warehouse across from the Burger King in the Regency Mall."

Geiger gave Fred several of his tattoos, including an inscription of Fred's name on the back of his arm. Fred's early bands, such as Authority Porch, Split 26, and 10 Foot Shindig, showcased a sound similar to the one Limp Bizkit would take to No. 1 a few years later. Geiger said, "It was relatively comparable, not so commercial. It was heavy, hip-hop oriented, kinda like Urban Dance Squad. They sounded like they do now, rock and rap with a Rage [Against the Machine] influence. The music they play now is more melodic than their early stuff."

Developing his vision of a band that combined elements of rock and rap was foremost on Fred's mind at this time. Devoting himself single-mindedly to finding the right players to join him, meant other aspects of his life went neglected. Fred lamented his lack of a relationship with his now 10-year-old daughter Adriana in an interview with *Rolling Stone*. "I was chasing the dreams. And it took a while to make that happen, to get the breaks. I really haven't been able to spend much time on the father-daughter thing. I think when she gets a little older, we're going to bond pretty good."

The disparity between Fred and Wes is best evidenced in their outside interests and outlets for creativity. For Fred, that meant tattooing. Geiger described Fred's tattoo style as "mainly graffiti art, new school," of the kind that adorns both of their records, while Wes's interests stray toward sewing and design. In an interview with *Maximum Guitar*, Wes discussed his anti–rock-star love of sewing. "I have two sewing kits and a 1940s Singer sewing machine in mint condition. They're just tools for whatever—I'm always doing weird projects. I was originally a visual artist, and my hobby was guitar, but I ended up getting a job in a band. I was always in bands, but I never thought it would amount to anything. Before we got signed, I was sending out my portfolio to art colleges—I was about to jet from the band."

As kids of a cop and a minister, Fred and Wes grew up differently, with different heros tapes and CDs cluttering their bedrooms but a couple collaborations in the 80s and 90s helped link rock with rap and clear the path for Limp Bizkit. Run-DMC's teaming with Aerosmith on "Walk This Way" broke ground in the now fertile rap-rock ground but combining the two had been mostly written off as a novelty until the pairing of Anthrax and Public Enemy on a blistering update of P.E.'s "Bring the

Noise." Unlike Fred, who hopped onboard the hip-hop ship early on and had immersed himself in the old school hip-hop of Grandmaster Flash and the Sugarhill Gang and made like Turbo and Ozone in junior high talent shows, Wes said it took hearing "Bring the Noise" to interest him. "All of the long-haired, heavy metal kids got introduced to the whole hip-hop world through Anthrax and the *Attack of the Killer B's* album [which features a collaboration with Public Enemy]. All of a sudden I realized, 'Wow! This is really cool stuff!' And I had heard of Public Enemy before, but it never really piqued my interest to the point of going out and buying a record until then."

When Wes's parents relocated to Jacksonville, he went along, and enrolled at the Douglas Anderson School of the Arts. Wes described the bleak Jacksonville scene of the early 90s to spinal-column.com. "There was like two scenes going on in our town in Jacksonville. Which one of the scenes was super—almost Sonic Youth-y type of Sebadoh, really indie-rock scene. Where all the guitars are going through two hundred effects pedals. Wall of noise type of bands. They all wore thrift store clothes . . . they looked really thin and sad. It was that scene, and there was another scene that was super heavy metal. Like ridiculous heavy metal."

Given the unhappy state of music in his hometown, it's not surprising that Wes thought he was going to make his mark in the oh-so-glamorous world of special effects. "I was there for sculpture and painting. The point of me going to art school was to one day get into special effects and monster makeup in film," Wes explained to *Maximum Guitar*. All my sculptures were these awful-looking, sci-fi, as-real-as-I-could-get-'em horrible creatures. I was in training in my own mind for something later on."

Mark Dobelstein, a classmate with Wes at Douglas Anderson, described a portrait of Wes as a young man in an interview with the *Florida Times-Union*. "Wes was kind of a goofball, a class clown, but a really nice guy. We had a sculpture class together, and I built this huge chicken wire and plastic sculpture that was about eight feet tall. It was a performance piece, and we beat it up with bats. I think he enjoyed doing that."

When not clobbering plastic sculptures with baseball bats, Wes was continuing to take guitar lessons, this time from a teacher specializing in jazz, who only learned that Wes couldn't read the music that he could play, by mistake. "My first teacher ingrained playing by ear so much that when my jazz teacher gave me a sheet of music and a tape to go with it, I would learn the tape instantly and go in and play it, but I couldn't make myself learn the music," said Wes to *Maximum Guitar*. For eight months I didn't learn a single note of music, until I made one mistake and he said, 'Stop. Play that note.' And I couldn't. I was tricking him the whole time."

Wes's parents tracked his progress as a visual artist and guitarist carefully. Like any concerned parent who watched their kid turn his back on the more stable fields of accounting or law in favor of a career as an artist, Wes's dad encouraged him to have a safety net, in case his foray into the world of music failed. His father knew firsthand about the disappointments that can come while attempting to pursue a career in the arts, having chased several promising leads for his own folk music into dead ends. "He was like, 'Well, we'd like you to have a fall-back plan,' " Wes said in an interview with *Guitar One*. "And I'm like, 'It doesn't really work like that, Dad. I've just got to go for it. I can't go to college and try to be playing at the same time— playing out with the band at the same time I'm trying to make straight As. It's one or the other.' "

As his skills with his six-string picked up, Wes shifted his focus from painting and sculpting to crafting guitar parts, integrating what he learned from other artistic pursuits into his songwriting. In an interview with *New Music Monthly*, Wes talked about how he enhances songs, forming them in rough outlines and then filling in the details later. "I'm good at creating ideas while using a guitar in a new way, but it takes me a long time. I can't just come up with stuff fast and rip it up. I think about constructing songs, and even riffs, in the same way as a painting, putting on a little bit at a time. They're sketchy at first, and then I know what I want, and I fit notes into places."

Although Wes and Fred had yet to meet, Fred would soon begin to assemble Limp Bizkit in the same way that Wes was writing songs. Beginning with the concept of a band that meshed metal and hip-hop into one, Fred would add pieces to his band, a little bit at a time, fitting players into places.

# Two

Fred's early bands flopped, with Split 26 never taking off, Malachi Sage steering clear of the charts, and 10 Foot Shindig destined to be known as the band that Fred Durst left to begin Limp Bizkit. From playing around town, Fred did learn what the music he wanted to make needed to sound like. Wes explained the recipe for Limp Bizkit as made by Fred.

"Fred had this idea for a megaband, where he'd have musicians who could cross over into as many different styles of music as possible and mix them all together," Wes said to *Maximum Guitar*. "So we were all adopted one by one. It started as a concept, and Fred went through everyone he knew to find the kind of people he wanted."

After another in a long line of memorable 10 Foot Shindig gigs, Fred approached bassist Sam Rivers who kept holding up the low end in Malachi

Sage after Fred left. "They were in other bands in Jacksonville. I was in this one alternative band called Malachi Sage, and Sam was the bass player," said Fred to allmusic.com. "The rest of the band wouldn't listen to what I said, so I said 'Fuck them' and started 10 Foot Shindig. Sam was still in Malachi Sage. One night they opened for us, and I went and saw Sam and said, 'You need to quit this band and start a band with me that's like this: rappin' and rockin'.'"

A professed fan of grunge and metal growing up, Sam is to the rock element of Limp Bizkit what DJ Lethal would come to represent from the hip-hop side of life. "I was totally into the Seattle scene," Sam said in an interview with MTV News. "I grew up in, like, metal. I was totally into Megadeth, rocking it hard. Thank God I grew out of it."

In a move that eventually became permanent, Sam suggested that his cousin John Otto, at the time studying jazz drumming at the Douglas Anderson School of the Arts and hitting the skins for the avant-garde juggernaut, that was the Matt Butler Quartet join the band. Still too young to vote or buy cigarettes when Sam recruited him for Limp Bizkit, John told *Drum!* he jumped at the chance. "He's like, 'Man, I got this singer [Durst], we're trying to start a band. Do you know any drummers that are good that want to do anything?' And I was like, 'Well, I'm not good, but I'll join the band.' It just all hooked-up and wham-bam, you have the worst band in the world."

Ace Martin, Department Chair of Instrumental Music and Jazz band director at Douglas Anderson, recalled John as a promising student who was his own biggest obstacle to success. "John always had a lot of potential, but I think his worst enemy was himself," Martin recalled to the *Florida Times-Union*. "He had tons of talent, and I sometimes wished he would have gone into another direction with his music. But he seems to be doing fine now. He got interested in other kinds of music during his senior year and stayed with it."

Even if Ace Martin isn't necessarily thrilled with the path picked by John Otto, he sufficiently impressed his new bandmates to keep the drummer's seat, long after his temporary stint was to have expired. Fred said the rudimentary lineup of Limp Bizkit began to gel almost immediately in an interview with allmusic.com. "The first day we jammed with John [Otto], and I was playing guitar and rapping and he was playing drums and Sam was on the bass, it happened right then. We wrote three songs, and there we were."

While at Douglas Anderson, John picked up solid fundamentals and learned to play a variety of percussive instruments, but in an interview with *Drum!* he said he always favored working with a plain old drum kit, over the more exotic timekeeping devices. "I've got a pretty extensive background in percussion and [at school] I was taking mostly straight-up [percussion]—everything from Brazilian and Afro-Cuban to straight bebop to funk to whatever. But I've gravitated more towards the drum set. I really just wanted to play the drum set and match that. I was never really into the percussion thing."

Wes Borland, who also did a stint at Douglas Anderson in addition to his twisted work in the visual arts, managed to convince Tom Haller, Director of Bands at Douglas Anderson, that no matter what Wes was up to, it would somehow involve making music. "I've got an archive tape of Wes singing that his fans would love to hear, but I do have my professional ethics," said Haller in the *Florida Times-Union*. "They were never afraid to do different things and see what would happen. These guys were going to play music no matter if they became famous or not."

Joining Limp Bizkit meant a couple different things for Wes. In all his previous bands he'd been the singer/guitarist of a three-piece, but joining Limp Bizkit meant he wouldn't be in the blinding glare of the spotlight as the band's frontman and that he would have to adapt his style of guitar to fit the sound that Fred was hearing in his head. The transition was sometimes difficult, with tensions once mounting to the point that Wes left the band, which he later dismissed to *Maximum Guitar* as "Two cocky roosters butting heads."

Even though Fred and Wes weren't always at loggerheads, it took time for Wes to adjust his play to fit the sound of Limp Bizkit. "I've always been the singer and guitarist in bands I've been in, and I've only been in three-pieces, with my brother being the bass player. Sam is the only other bass player I've ever worked with. For Limp Bizkit, I've had to hold back so much because I'm used to the three-piece, where we all had to fill more listening space up. Here, there's so much going on. They're going, 'No, no, no. Not that much.' "

As any member of the Goo Goo Dolls will tell you, a band's name should be chosen with caution. Pick a bad one and you'll be going onstage the rest of your life as Deep Blue Something. In choosing a name that the members of Limp Bizkit agreed was a bad one, the band was looking to beat critics to the punch by purposefully picking the worst imaginable handle. The most common story circulated to explain the origin of the Limp Bizkit moniker says the name was initially an adjective applied by Fred to describe a dim roadie's brain. In the band's bio, Fred discussed the strategy behind the selection of the Limp Bizkit name. "The name is there to turn people's heads away. A lot of people pick up the disc and go, 'Limp Bizkit. Oh, they must suck.' Those are the people that we don't even want listening to our music."

Stateside, the Limp Bizkit name just looks misspelled with a possible impaired phallic reference but overseas Limp Bizkit takes on a completely new, and sometimes obscene connotation. "We've heard that in Australia there's a game called soggy biscuit, but they call it limp biscuit, too. It's played by teenage boys, and they have a circle jerk on a biscuit or a piece of bread, and whoever comes last has to eat the bread. That should make things interesting when we play there."

When initial contacts with labels came around to the topic of their name, Limp Bizkit received a great deal of pressure to come up with something better, but Wes said seeing the record company resistance to their handle only hardened their resolve to stick with it. "When all the record companies were becoming interested in us, they wanted us to change the name—they all thought it was terrible, and they probably made a lot of other bands change their names," Wes said to *Guitar One*. "So we went, 'No way! We're definitely not going to change it now!'"

As any band worth the cover charge and the time it takes them to watch them knows, live gigs are where a band finds out if the hours spent in dingy practice rooms perfecting parts and arguing about ideas, matters to anybody that isn't in the band. When Limp Bizkit first started playing out, they were confined to the Green Room in the Milk Bar, a smallish room with a capacity of close to 150.

When early shows failed to fill the room, Fred's entrepreneurial skills began to surface and the crowds swelled as word of mouth began to make people curious to see the band that covered George Michael's "Faith" and Paula Abdul's "Straight Up" in concert.

Fred acknowledged that the early shows weren't exactly a tough ticket to come by, but he told the *L.A. Times* that after the band's first show, he knew he'd hit on a combo that would far outstrip the legendary output of his earlier outfits, such as Malachi Sage and 10 Foot Shindig. "There were only about thirty people there, but something happened that night. Our energy and presence—it was just like, 'Oh my God, we've got something here.'" Limp Bizkit eventually left the cozy Green Room at the Milk Bar behind, when they graduated to the main stage.

Wes applied his art-school background to the Limp Bizkit stage show, appearing live in an array of costumes that seem at odds with the throw-your-hands-in-the-air vibe of the hip-hop side of the band. Tapping into the theatrical aspect of rock gave fans one more reason to head out to 128 West Adams in Jacksonville and watch Limp Bizkit rock the hiz-ouse. "It's just a lot more fun to dress up and look completely bizarre onstage. Keep it different. It's grown to be different characters, now. Like, I have a bunny suit, and a skeleton suit, and this big, oversized kung fu suit that I wear onstage,"

Wes said to *Guitar*, before going on to describe his latest outfit, the Burnt Match. "I go onstage wearing almost nothing. I have underwear and my boots on, and I paint my whole head black from the neck up and I have the black contacts. All you can see is these glowing teeth."

Danny Wimmer, owner of the since-closed Milk Bar and a friend of the band who was thanked in the liner notes of both Limp Bizkit records, described the club where Limp Bizkit cut their live teeth. "It was considered the CBGB's of Florida," he modestly declared. "It was an underground club that was literally underground in a basement. Everybody played there, 311, Korn, Pennywise, the Sugar Ray/Deftones package tour. We were the kings of punk rock. Every single established punk rock band played here."

Fred's dad, more familiar with shutting down concerts and keeping noise to a minimum during his twenty-two-year career as a cop, braved all the young dudes and attended an early show at the Milk Bar. "I'm pretty cynical from being a cop for so many years. The first time I went to see them at the Milk Bar, there was so much energy in the audience, all the kids moved like one person out there," he said in an interview with the *Florida Times-Union*. "I said to myself, these guys have a real shot."

Wimmer said Limp Bizkit's local draw was such that Sugar Ray opened for Limp Bizkit before Limp

Bizkit was signed. "They had the biggest draw for a local band. They went from playing to like ten people to eight hundred within months. Fred was just the genius marketing guy. It was incredible. He's so in touch with the kids. They used to play George Michael's 'Faith' and Paula Abdul's 'Straight Up.' He was always marketing the band. He would go to record stores and get people involved, he was in touch with high schools."

Of a September 3, 1995 show in the 1,400-capacity Milk Bar with Less Than Jake, before either band had broken nationally, Wimmer said simply, "It was slam-packed." Jason Lewis, booker for the Milk Bar, was most impressed by the exponential nature of Limp Bizkit's draw, and told the *Florida Times-Union* that even early on it looked like Limp Bizkit had a shot at the big time. "They had charisma. They were tight. They'd bring out more people every time they'd play," he recalled after the release of *Significant Other*. "Every month, their crowd would double. I knew they had what it took to be something," he said. "They're actual rock stars now. Girls scream their names, and little kids run down the street trying to get their autographs."

What made Limp Bizkit's success in playing live particularly remarkable has a lot to do with the Jacksonville music scene, or lack thereof. Since the craze over Lynyrd Skynyrd, Molly Hatchet, and .38 Special died down, the city of Jacksonville has had little to crow about. Without any acts to put them on the map and without the "I'll scratch your back, you scratch my back" attendance that bands can get from other bands, Limp Bizkit knew if they were going to graduate to the national level, their live show would have to be something special. "Well, there's a lot of good bands [in Jacksonville], but there's no scene," said Wes in *Maximum Guitar*. "There are good bands for a totally different reason, which I think maybe sometimes makes the lyrics more real—or the emotions in the band more real— because they have nothing: they have a bar to play at where someone is yelling 'Play Molly Hatchet' in the background."

Wimmer remembers the early Limp Bizkit shows at the Milk Bar as chaos in motion and said the band would be hard pressed to match the intensity generated years ago in the underground club. "When they played our place they'd go off. They don't jump around like they used to. They don't go off as hard. Wes would be on the guitar speakers, Sam would be jumping around. Fred would be jumping off the stage and into the crowd, although Fred still goes out into the crowd. Wes always used to have pigtails. He would wear these snowboard boots of all his own design and he'd be on stage in his underwear, pigtails, and snow boots."

Fred's "genius marketing guy" status went beyond cramming the kids into clubs to catch the live show in his off-hours from his career as a tattoo artist. Fred also took to cold-calling record companies bluffing that Limp Bizkit was big-time, in the hopes of getting the right eyes or right ears to check them out on tour. "I would call up A&R [Artists and Repertoire] people at all these different labels and pretend to be the band's manager," Durst said in a June 1997 interview with the *Florida Times-Union*, just before the release of *Three Dollar Bill Y'all*. "I would say something like, 'I manage this great band called Limp Bizkit, and they're going to be playing at such and such a place, and you need to catch them.' I called everybody—Columbia, Jive, everybody. I b.s.'ed, basically."

Despite all of Fred's best attempts at hustling Limp Bizkit a record deal, their big break didn't come until Korn came to town. Accounts vary of the night in question, but the general consensus is that Korn opened for Sick Of It All, Fred did some fast talking, and wound up having Korn over for some beers and bad tattoos.

"I had only been tattooing for like a couple weeks and I lied to 'em and told him I'd been tattooing for like a long time. . . . We were drunk, they were drunk. . . . They fell for it and it got them back to the house," said Fred in an interview on *Modern Rock Live*. "I drew up this thing that said 'Korn' and it kinda looks like 'Horn' but Fieldy was so wasted he was like 'Yeah, man, let's do it' and that was that. And everybody wants to rag me about it ever since then."

Without impressing anyone with his tattoo abilities Fred managed to get the band's tape in Fieldy's hands during Korn's next swing through the Sunshine State. Fieldy gave the three-song demo—consisting of "Pollution," "Counterfeit," and "Stuck"—to Ross Robinson, a producer from California who had been behind the boards for Korn's first two records and was rapidly becoming the producer of choice for Adidas rock acts. Limp Bizkit's friendship with Korn would prove to be a valuable one, as Korn were a couple records ahead of them and had enough clout to bring them on two tours before they were signed and enough fans to help give Limp Bizkit a new audience. Like most good things, Limp Bizkit's alliance with Korn had a flipside and it would take two records and touring across a couple continents to get completely clear of Korn's long shadow. According to Korn singer Jonathan Davis, discovering Limp Bizkit and watching them take off, prompted them to start their own Elementree label. "Because of what we did with Limp Bizkit," Davis explained to MTV. "Finding them, getting them phat, taking them on the road with us for as long as we did. And we were like, 'Fuck, we should have signed them to our own label.' "

Even before Limp Bizkit began, DJ Lethal found success of the platinum kind as a DJ with House of Pain. With a heavily pro-Irish image and the kind of tunes that made the kids want to jump up, jump up and get down, House of Pain's biggest hit was the party anthem "Jump Around." The hits after "Jump Around" were few and far between and on the day House of Pain's third LP, *Truth Crushed to Earth Shall Rise Again* came out, the lead singer, Everlast, considered the rigors of another year on the road and decided he wanted out. In an interview with *Top* magazine Everlast explained the reason for House of Pain's untimely demise. "House of Pain had become a product that was more about the image of the group than anything else, and I was becoming more and more unhappy. When we put out our last record, they were talking about a year's worth of touring, and I think that subconsciously I feared for my health. I had to quit, change the tempo, and find myself."

With his gigs as the Latvian guy in the Irish band ended, DJ Lethal found himself free to explore new opportunities. Having toured with Limp Bizkit while with House of Pain, Lethal was familiar with their music, and soon he and the other four members of Limp Bizkit were sitting down and talking about how he would fit with the band and what he could bring to the table.

Limp Bizkit had experimented with a keyboard player and off and on thought of adding a second guitarist, and began listening closely as they got to know DJ Lethal and some of the ideas he had for applying his DJ skills within the context of a rock band. "He told us how he wanted to do more than just play DAT tapes and scratch. He had all these crazy ideas about running MPCs and turntables through wah-wah pedals and envelope filters, and he wanted to go through a Marshall amp," said Fred to *Musician*. "When they broke up, I told him, 'Fuck that, Holmes, you're coming with us.' "

A failed audition by a potential guitarist cemented Wes's belief that another guitar wasn't the answer but the addition of Lethal's new dimension provided the added sound the band sought without the friction another guitar player would have caused. "They were talking about bringing another guitar player in. There was one practice with him. And I went, 'Nope,' and that was it. Lee is like another guitar player who is not a guitar player," said Wes in *Maximum Guitar*. "He runs his turntables through a Marshall stack with distortion. He'd never really been a DJ in a rock band before, so in the end the way he thinks about it is, we're his other turntable."

Part of the first generation to grow up listening to both rock and rap, Lethal's CD collection had a lot of overlap with the rest of the guys in the band, and like the others enjoyed a great deal of exposure to music as a kid. "I grew up with a lot of hip-hop," Lethal said in an MTV interview. "Basically that's about it. My dad's a musician too, he plays the guitar so I was brought up with everything ... from

Stevie Wonder to . . . you name it. I mean, I just grew up with music so I always just had a wide variety of everything. But mostly hip-hop and old classic rock and stuff."

Joining Limp Bizkit for DJ Lethal also meant an opportunity to experiment with his turntable technique in ways that straight hip-hop doesn't allow for. In an interview with *Musician* magazine Lethal talked about the additional flexibility available to him in a rock band. "For hip-hop, it doesn't really matter," he says. "You don't have to worry about keys; it's just scratching [spoken] word records. You've got the vocals and everything set to one tune, so you don't have to worry about anything but a DAT machine, so you scratch during the choruses and pick your nose during the verses [while] two guys run around. It's all right, but it gets tired after a while. This is totally different energy. You've got to adapt to it."

As the band came together, the elements that would help Limp Bizkit forge a sound apart from the traditional guitar, bass, and drums began to gel. Lethal's time spinning the wheels of steel with House of Pain had given him a taste of success and an idea of what the big time is all about. Rather than come in and try and force his turntable work on the band's sound, Lethal opted to add accents and ultimately function as the second guitar that Wes's brother used to provide.

A brief bidding war for Limp Bizkit's services erupted after a showcase opening for Korn at the Dragonfly in Hollywood went well and the band ultimately opted to sign with Mojo, a subsidiary with MCA. The band, minus Wes, who had left the band after a disagreement with Fred, set out to California to make their record. But in the early morning hours on a lonely stretch of Interstate 10, just outside the booming metropolis of Van Horn, Texas, the band's van flipped in a wreck that would greatly alter their future. "We were asleep, and the driver fell asleep at six in the morning in the middle of the desert," Fred recalled to allmusic.com. "He had over-rotated and tried to correct it. The van flipped five or six times. We were all asleep, falling out of the windows. My feet got crushed. Everybody got banged and cut up. One guy who came along with us broke his back and was just lying in the street in the freezing cold desert. It was a big lesson for all to learn."

The wreck rocked Fred and made him reconsider his fleeting vision of a Limp Bizkit without Wes Borland. Seeing the accident as a sign, Fred swallowed his pride and made the call. "I suddenly thought, 'This is my chance—I'm taking this as karma. It was kind of like God flipping the van. We took it as a sign to get Wes back and start all over again." In bringing back Wes, Limp Bizkit restored Fred's foil to the fold, the artistic counterpoint to Fred's terrierlike ambition, and a personality strong enough to butt heads with Fred when necessary. In talking about the split and his relationship with Wes, Fred told *Spin* that life with Wes sometimes drove him nuts but life without him was bad. "[Wes] is cool, but we have different tastes. I just couldn't deal with him at one point. . . . [But there] wasn't anyone as good as him who I liked as much. So now he's the guy who makes us listen to Ween on the tour bus."

In addition to providing the impetus to get Wes back in the band, the wreck on that empty Texas interstate also fulfilled an eerie prophecy made by the band before leaving Florida for California. "Before the car wreck, we were on our way out to California, and we said the only way we won't be on Mojo is if we flipped the van or something," said Fred to allmusic.com. "It was weird."

A dispute with Mojo led to Limp Bizkit seeking the help of Jordan Schur, president of the Interscope distributed subsidiary, Flip Records. Prior to Limp Bizkit's signing with Mojo, Schur actively courted the band, terming them "unfuckupable," the closest thing to a sure shot the fickle music industry had to offer. Part of Limp Bizkit's excitement at signing with Flip stemmed from the fact that Flip had a distribution deal with Interscope and execs at Interscope were offering an open-door policy. "We were talking to nothing but A&R guys at Mojo," Fred told the *Florida Times-Union*. "We wanted to be in a situation where we could talk to the head of the label whenever we wanted. At Interscope, we can dial up [president] Jimmy Iovine any time." Rather than spurn the band the way they initially did him, Schur worked with them and ultimately bought out their contract from Mojo and added Limp Bizkit to the Flip roster.

Danny Wimmer remembers Fred and Wes being exuberant during their first meeting with Jordan Schur, and was present when the Flip Records exec first heard the band that would help make his fledgling label nationally known. Wimmer said he and Florida promoter Fat Harry arranged a meeting between Jordan, Fred, and Wes, which ultimately led to Limp Bizkit signing with Flip Records. "Jordan came down there and they'd brought this demo tape," Wimmer said. "We listened to it in our car. Fred and Wes were outside. Fred was rapping as it was playing and Wes was jumping around and playing air guitar."

One of the songs Limp Bizkit arrived at Indigo Ranch with had fallen into the Bizkit basket courtesy of the Jacksonville music scene. Fusing hip-hop and rock had become Limp Bizkit's trademark on Florida's First Coast and the band did not react kindly when they realized that it was being infringed upon. In an interview with the web site Spinal Column in October 1997 Wes said that "Counterfeit" has its origins in the band's frustration at finding other acts copping their sound. "They saw this little thing we built, or whatever, and they went and they were like, 'Oh, let's get baggy pants and dress like kind of hip-hoppy and, you know, play heavy metal and rap.' And then we went, 'Holy shit! What's going on here?' Like five or six bands just popped up out of nowhere that became these, you know, groups that were trying to sound like us. It was ridiculous. That's where the song 'Counterfeit' came from."

When it came time to record the record, Limp Bizkit turned to Ross Robinson, whose work with Korn and the Deftones impressed the band. Robinson said Fieldy from Korn gave him Limp Bizkit's demo tape and then the phone calls began. "Fieldy gave Fred my phone number. Fred kept calling me and bugging me asking me if I got the tape and he'd call like three or four times a day to see if I'd listened to it yet. I gave it to my girlfriend and she listened to it and gave it the thumbs up."

Danny Wimmer, owner of the Milk Bar, said he spent about a week visiting and hanging out with the band during the recording of their first record and remembers Indigo Ranch for its stunning setting. "Indigo Ranch is up on this hill. You can see the Pacific from there and there's canyons all around it. It's got the greatest vibe. It's a real old studio, it's real classic stuff. . . . It's got cabins where bands can stay, you can go mountain biking and hiking up in the hills, those were some great nights."

Robinson said the band worked each day from one in the afternoon until eleven at night, laboring tirelessly to capture the sound they'd cultivated from playing live and practicing. During the hours spent recording each day, Robinson came away impressed by the band's motivation and their instrumental acumen. "They were on fire. They're supertalented. Every player was just amazing. Their hearts were fucking hungry and I love that. It's like there was no drama or anything, it was just about having a killer time mashing tracks onto tape."

Nearly three years after producing *Three Dollar Bill Y'all*, the record that would put Limp Bizkit on the map, Robinson's memories of the off-hours from recording vary from a grab bag of experiences to moments between Fred and his girlfriend that would foreshadow events and songs to come. "I remember Lethal and Sam smoking cigs. It was wintertime and there was lots of wind and Fred was on the phone with his girlfriend doing drama every single second. Wes and I hanging out and having a great time. Those guys going to strip clubs and getting strippers to come back up. They're not really, like, players, but a roadie guy and Fred had a flow of girls in here. Citrus wars in the orchard out here. We would throw citrus at each other and just have a good time. I love it. I like thinking of it and when

I hear the record I'm grateful I could help any way I could."

The phone drama between Fred and his girlfriend, Robinson recalls, immediately inspired "Sour" and would later inspire "Nookie." Fred said in the Q&A released by the label with the first record that the situation between himself and his girlfriend came to a head during the recording of the record and it was then that he ended the relationship. "Every time we'd get into a crazy argument, she'd say so many things to hurt me and I'd get upset and snap. I just couldn't take it anymore. . . . Finally, I realized in my world I don't need that. I'm just insecure like that. I want to be with someone, I need that part in my life to be fulfilled and finally I just said, 'Get your bags and hit the trail.' We recorded that song at the studio while all of this was going on."

After a couple years as a band, Limp Bizkit had a slew of tunes ready to record, but when luck landed in their laps, in the form of the improvised song "Everything," the band happily accepted the gift. "I had my band, I had Ross, we had candles. We were just improvising. You miss about five minutes of the intro because we were improvising and I was just feeling it. I was, like, crying. We were like going off. Ross ran into the studio and said 'Richard, record this,'" said Fred in the Q&A released with the record. "So he recorded us improvising. That's just how we were feeling so that's total improv. We never played that song before you heard it on that tape."

Improvisations such as the ones that yielded "Everything" were made possible in part by the mood and tone set by Robinson in the studio. In an interview with spinalcolumn.com in October of '97, Wes talked about what made Robinson such a tight fit for Limp Bizkit. "Ross is such a great producer. He's so easy to work with. He's a vacuum cleaner for emotion. He just sucks it out of you . . . and brings it out and puts it on tape. He brought stuff out in all of us that we didn't really even know was in there, but it was. That's more than a producer. He's a really good motivator/instigator. He really just pulls out melody and fear and love, aggression."

Recording the album gave Limp Bizkit a chance to showcase the addition of DJ Lethal. "I bring a bunch of crap to the table," said Lethal in an interview with the web site Wall of Sound. "Seriously, though, as far as Limp Bizkit goes, I try and bring new sounds, not just the regular chirping scratching sounds. You won't really hear the regular, been-there-done-that scratching, know what I mean? It's all different stuff that you haven't heard before. I'm trying to be like another guitar player. That's my main goal."

Wes talked about what the addition of Lethal added to the band in an October 1997 interview with Spinal Column. "I think that playing-wise, we really complement each other in the songs. One of the goals on the record that we were trying to strive for was to have there be certain parts of the record where you couldn't tell what was the DJ and what was the guitar. I think we achieved that in some way. There are parts on the records where people come up to me all the time going, "Is that guitar or is that . . . ?"

The guitar sounds that are actually guitar sounds on *Three Dollar Bill Y'all*, include some tricks employed by Wes that were staples of his days in previous bands when he was the lone guitarist and needed to take up more sonic space in the mix. "In my last band, I wasn't even using a pick at all. I was doing all playing with two hands, one doing melody, the other doing chord progressions," Wes said in an interview with *Maximum Guitar*. "You'll hear that on the record on 'Stalemate' and 'Sour' and 'Indigo Glow.' I get to do it a little bit, but I've had to go back to using a pick."

Although most people agree that Limp Bizkit's cover of George Michael's "Faith" helped them make the leap from well-traveled road dogs to a bonafide bankable act, producer Ross Robinson said that when the band first proposed committing their spin on the tune to tape, he was completely opposed to the idea. "When they told me they wanted to cover 'Faith,' I didn't like it and I asked if they were sure they wanted to do it and they were, so I said 'all right.' They worked hard on it and it turned out great. The DJ thing at the end is magic to me. Those guys know how to turn it on and that's pretty rare."

The tune that George Michael popularized over a decade earlier relied on an acoustic guitar and Michael's suggestive crooning to get its lusty message across, but when Limp Bizkit decided to cover the song, they went out of their way to make it their own. The heavier guitars and drums were pretty much a given but Fred said in the Q&A released with the record, that the updated song's greatest change came as part of a spontaneous moment in the studio. "It's just one of those covers that I've always wanted to do. Instead of saying what I was supposed to say in the middle of the song, I screamed 'Get the fuck up!' Everybody was sitting down in the studio when I was recording the song and I looked at everybody and said it and everybody got up and started jumping and moshing in the studio, right in the vocal room. It was awesome, man."

Robinson described Fred as a go-getter, eager to advance his career and the band's while Wes serves as the clown prince of the band, with his unique appreciation of the absurd and fickle nature of the music industry. "Wes and I connected," Robinson said. "He thinks it's all a joke because it really is. He's not really into the band or the rock and roll thing at all. He's just there because he's supposed to do it. I don't think he takes Limp Bizkit seriously. He likes to goof around, like what you have with his funny faces. You can tell what Wes does. It's pretty obvious he's a genius, he's such a genius he's bored with it."

The recording and release of *Three Dollar Bill Y'all* provided the first window into Fred's angry psyche, with songs such as "Nobody Loves Me" that explore Fred's 'I'll hit you back' mentality. In a Q&A sent out with the band's bio Fred discussed the idea behind "Nobody Loves Me." "When my mom used to ground me and I got upset, she'd say, 'Oh, nobody loves me, I'm going to go eat worms.' So it was like this saying that I used to get pounded with by my mother. She had this little cross-stitch on the wall that said 'Nobody loves me, everybody hates me, I think I'll go eat worms.' Here's how I look at it: since nobody loves me, I don't owe you a thing."

Professed fans of Tool, Fred told MTV that their influence shines through in the Limp Bizkit song "Nobody Loves Me" where Fred cops Maynard's singing style. "You listen to his words, and you're like, 'Holy shit, how did you write that song?' And he sings in ways that . . . like you can hear the influence of Maynard in the [Limp Bizkit] song 'Nobody Loves Me' in the middle, in the breakdown in the middle. I actually copied the way he sings."

In writing the lyrics for *Three Dollar Bill Y'all* Fred helped establish Limp Bizkit's direction and audience. Rather than write for the kind of indie kids that spend their days and nights wearing thrift-store sweaters and hanging out in crowded coffee-houses hotly debating Marxist theory, Fred aimed his lyrical darts at a more easily attainable target. "We like to write songs about things we can relate to," Fred said in an interview with *Hit Parader*. "That's why a song like 'Counterfeit' is about all the fake people who change their selves and what they really believe in, just so they can fit in with the people they think are cool. . . . A song like 'Pollution' speaks about all the people who always say that music like ours is nothing but noise pollution. There's nothing particularly heavy there—no big-time message."

In a Q&A with Fred for *Three Dollar Bill Y'all*, Fred elaborated on the idea that prompted him to write the lyrics for "Pollution," a corrosively angry tune aimed at the perceived hypocrites in his life. "Instead of saying you preach the words about the noise you don't want to hear, I say you preach the noise about the words you don't want to hear. It's like, well, you're preaching and telling me that I'm so wrong—well, that's noise to me because little do you know that my band says a prayer every time before they go on stage and we're not just praying to Buddha or something."

Named after the studio, "Indigo Flow" was Limp Bizkit's thank you to the assortment of people who made their dream of playing music professionally a reality. In a Q&A with Fred released with the record, he rattled off a list of people that got props in the tune. "I gave a shout out to Fat Harry Tyler, a big promoter here in Florida. I gave a shout out to Cheetah, 'Line 'Em Up Cheetah'—the dog at Indigo Ranch where we recorded the record. Richard, Rob, and Chuck were the engineers at Indigo Ranch. Ross Robinson, he's our producer. My mom and dad. Sage, my girlfriend." As Wes explained to the *Iowa State Daily*, the more traditional route of a thank you in the liner notes just didn't quite seem to do the trick. "So many people have done so much, we had to write a song to thank them. We thanked them in the liner notes, but they deserve more than that."

The completed *Three Dollar Bill Y'all* took on an abrasive, angry tone which Wes told launch.com was part of Limp Bizkit's plan to get noticed. "That's what we find works best for us. The best way to get our message across is through shock value. That's what grabs people. I mean, you turn on the TV and you see a bunch of starving children in another country and it gets you to react, and that's kind of what we're about, getting people to react by showing something negative, hoping something positive will come out of it. Trying to stay in reality."

Beyond playing under a name that each member of Limp Bizkit thinks is dumb, the Bizkit bunch took their policy of advancement-by-repulsion a step further with the naming of their record. Combining the saying "queer as a three dollar bill" with the downhome Florida flavor of "y'all," they came up with the title for their debut album.

Following the recording of the record, Limp Bizkit went out on tour with Korn and Helmet. In what would become a hallmark of Limp Bizkit's experience in the coming years, fans ate it up and critics regurgitated it back up. In the *Milwaukee Journal-Sentinel*, critic Jon M. Gilbertson took swipes at both Korn and Limp Bizkit. Korn, he said, "Comes across like someone beating you senseless while weeping about his pain," while his only mention of Limp Bizkit was a pointed critique of a comment Fred made from the stage. "The one attention-grabbing moment of Limp Bizkit's rap/thrash show was when the lead singer expressed a desire for gay men to be 'stomped.' Which isn't remotely rebellious. It's just puerile."

Interscope President Tom Whalley saw something different than what Jon M. Gilbertson saw. "It's not as if Limp were an overnight success," Whalley told *Spin*. "They toured forever. What was most exciting about those earlier shows was that you could tell that there was this new audience out there, kids in Adidas who were into both rock and rap—Korn's audience. We felt that Limp represented something that was going to happen in music on a larger scale."

# Three

In making the leap from an act that records albums and tours endlessly in anonymity, to the rank of superstar, a band needs one big break, to bump them up to the next level. Often it's a blend of good timing and dumb luck and a matter of getting the stars and moons aligned. The Bizkit boys aren't exactly the crystals and voodoo types, so it's not surprising that when Interscope approached them with a plan to pay the Portland radio station $5,000 to guarantee fifty spins of "Counterfeit," there was little opposition. Technically aired as an ad, with an announcement before and after the song that it was a paid advertisement from Interscope Records, the arrangement immediately drew scrutiny from the *New York Times* and similarly established media outlets, crying payola. Band manager Jeff Kwatinetz dismissed the claims at the time in an interview with the Addicted To Noise web site. "When you have a band like Limp Bizkit, who sell out 3,000-seaters, playing music the kids want to hear, finding a way to get them on a radio station without prostituting them is a huge plus for everybody," said Kwatinetz. "That song is still on KUFO because the song is a hit. The album has sold 170,000 copies, and Portland represents less than one percent of those sales."

Kwatinetz went on to term it a brilliant marketing move, that made money for the radio station and provided Limp Bizkit with the increased exposure they were seeking. In retrospect, given the flurry of media attention given to the band in the wake of the ad, the $5,000 Interscope paid to get "Counterfeit" some additional airtime, might well be the cheapest and most effective promotion in recent memory.

Kwatinetz said that the difference between payola and the ads Interscope placed centered around the fact that listeners were informed that the Limp Bizkit song was a paid ad and not played as though it were a DJ selection. "It's a very honest thing. There's nothing hidden about it," Kwatinetz continued. "If kids didn't want to hear the song, it would be off the air faster than you could say 'KUFO' . . . Payola was about DJs defrauding the owners of their stations and potentially hurting ratings by not making musical decisions. Then the FCC required people to say that a spin was paid for, so the fraud element was taken out of it. By us saying 'This is brought to you by Interscope,' you know the money is going to the station. If stations want to make bad decisions, then their ratings go down."

Dave Numme, operating manager of KUFO in Portland, Oregon, hailed the scratch for spins deal as good for the record labels in an interview with *Billboard* online. "It's a more efficient use of money for the record companies," Numme says. Promotional funds are usually used for "getting the record promoted to the [stations' program directors]. This would take the money and get the record to the audience."

Reaction from the band has been mixed. In interviews, Fred alternately sounds pleased with the results and somewhat chagrined at the means necessary to obtain them. "It worked, but it's not that cool of a thing. Some stations won't play your shit even though kids want it, so we had to pay to get 'em to play it. We were on the cover of the *New York Times*. It couldn't have been better, I was like, 'Ah! What the fuck did I do?' But the name Limp Bizkit got on MTV; it got in the paper. Even after the [paid radio] time expired, we stayed at number one."

In an interview with *Spin*, Fred took a more philosophical approach, "I mean, hey, they ended up playing the shit out of the record. It wasn't like we were getting tons of radio play anyway." Interscope president echoed Kwatinetz's sentiments in the same *Spin* article. "The station approached us.

They explained it was buying advertising time, not actual station time. We said, 'Sure, why not.' "

Now that Limp Bizkit show up on the cover of magazines like *Spin* with the kind of regularity that makes death and taxes look like uncertainties, it seems strange to think there was a time they had to pay to get their music heard. But in an interview with the web site Spinal Column in October 1997, only a few months before the pay-for-play brouhaha broke, Wes painted a picture of a band still waiting for their big break. "We've not had a lot of help from radio. We've had nothing on MTV. I think MTV2 has maybe played our video twice. The Box has played it, but the Box is only regional. And Canada's Much Music has done a little bit with it. But, for the most part, by chance you might catch it being played. It's not a regular thing."

Interscope president Tom Whalley later told *Billboard* online that paying to get "Counterfeit" on the radio in Portland didn't do nearly as much for Limp Bizkit as touring did. "We were approached by the station, and we tried it. It was such a minor thing in the two-year period of developing Limp Bizkit. I think touring was the main factor in why this band broke."

Even if the ad placed by Interscope had failed, Limp Bizkit was still sitting pretty in the catbird seat with the perfect trump card up their sleeves. Given the outpouring of 80s nostalgia that dominated the 90s, Limp Bizkit's choice to cover George

Michael's smash hit, with a thundering version of their own was a slam dunk. Keeping "Faith" as their ace in the hole played a central role in Limp Bizkit's plan to take the charts by storm. As Fred explained to the web site Addicted To Noise in January 1999, waiting for the opportune time to release "Faith" would give fans a chance to appreciate the band's sound minus the gimmick and "Faith" would be the hook to grab those who hadn't yet jumped onboard the Bizkit bandwagon. "We always knew it would be great, and our fans loved it, but we'd never put it out as the first single because we wanted more credibility than that. We worked singles and did it right and came out with 'Faith' as our last single. We knew it was going to do good, but we had no idea it would do what it's doing. This is a dream come true for a band."

Limp Bizkit's debut LP *Three Dollar Bill Y'all* came out and barely registered a ripple on the sales charts. With little fanfare greeting the arrival of their LP, Limp Bizkit began over a year-long siege of near constant touring, spending the summer on the punk-flavored Warped Tour with bands such as Pennywise, Mighty Mighty Bosstones, Sick Of It All, Lagwagon, and Blink 182.

Unlike some bands whose studio wizardry can't be recreated live without a full orchestra or a room with perfect acoustics, Limp Bizkit's sound translates easily to their live show. In an interview with the web site Spinal Column, Wes recounted the band's philosophy for playing to living and breathing humans. "There's nothing on the record we can't do live. And it's interesting because there's so much. . . . A lot of the stuff we did on the record was really spontaneous. So there's parts in the songs where we can really open it up and have fun with it live, and improv, and do different stuff. So it never gets boring to keep playing the songs live."

Touring with a DJ meant that Lethal and John had to take the additional challenge of keeping their sounds in sync. Having seen rap bands fall flat in attempting to incorporate live drums with the turntables, John told *Drum!* that getting familiar with Lethal's contributions is crucial to reproducing the tracks live. "It's the worst when you're not locked up with a loop. I've seen regular rap acts that play with a DAT, and then they have a live drummer. When the snares don't hit together, it's just the most awful thing to hear. . . . Lethal taught me how to program beats and use samplers, so I have a really good basis of where he's coming from as well."

With sales of *Three Dollar Bill Y'all* stagnant, it became obvious Limp Bizkit would have to build their fan base the old-fashioned way. Eaaaaaarn it. In the year following the release of *Three Dollar Bill Y'all* Limp Bizkit toured Europe twice, opened for Primus, opened for the Deftones, and headlined their own "Ladies Night in Cambodia" club tour before landing a slot on the Ozzfest. In an interview with allmusic.com, Fred expounded on why Limp

Bizkit needed to log nearly a year of club dates on the road to break through. "You gotta tour your ass off. You have to with our kind of band, because we're not major pop radio stars or rap stars. We're like a mixture in between. There are so many ups and downs to the band—a roller-coaster ride. You just have to tour and play in front of a lot of people, and then they realize you have a great show, and they get your record."

The "Ladies Night in Cambodia" tour featuring Limp Bizkit, Sevendust, and Clutch included an elaborate stage set-up with an empty Jeep, camouflage mesh, and palm trees adorning the stage in a juxtaposition of Limp Bizkit's desire to bolster their sagging female attendance and Fred's desire to pay his own peculiar homage to "Apocalypse Now," with a hint of reference to the Dead Kennedys thrown in for spice/cred.

Beginning February 24 in Lancaster, Pennsylvania and ending April 4 at Ziggy's in Winston-Salem, N.C., "The Ladies Night in Cambodia" tour was the band's first as a headliner and typified Limp Bizkit's awareness of their buying public. In the interests of diversifying their mostly male audience, the concept of letting the first two hundred women in free worked well with the wallets and went a long way to expanding Limp Bizkit's appeal. Besides nearly guaranteeing at least two hundred people in attendance each night, letting the ladies in gratis showed some understanding of the need to cater to one's audience.

Ziggy's owner and booker Jay Stephens called Limp Bizkit's "Ladies Night" promotion a first and raved about the show in his nine hundred–capacity club on the tour's final night. "Our stage is kind of small . . . they backed their eighteen-wheeler up to the club but there were a few props they could not use. They got a lot of stuff onstage. The netting around the speakers looked really good, the camoflouage, all the other stuff they needed but the Jeep. It was a great show, way energetic . . . lots of good-looking girls, lots of good positive energy. We gave away those tickets at the Record Exchange and all the tickets were picked up within the first two hours. I thought it was a great promotion, it was the first time a band decided to give away that many tickets in a house our size."

Circling Europe for the first time made an impression on Wes, who came home awed at the intensity of the audiences and the extremes to which they took their body art. In an interview with the web site Spinal Column in October 1997, Wes described the well-decorated fans at stops in Italy, France, Holland, Switzerland, and the U.K. "Those guys . . . you can take the biggest, nastiest, gnarliest person in the States, like a big huge punk three hundred–pound motherfucker . . . and he would just be dwarfed by the intensity of the guys over there. There were people who had those spike implants in their head. It won't be long before it's cool to cut your fingers off or something like that. It's unreal.

Like little girls with scarification, branded tattoos, and stuff. A little intense."

The European tour was memorable for Fred for reasons that go deeper than seeing some overly intense fans for the first time or catching a glimpse of the sights in Europe's historic capital cities. Having grossly overestimated his cash flow he found himself out of money and at the mercy of the better-funded members of Korn for means of getting more. As with all good friends, the guys in Korn were happy to kick down some cash, in exchange for a little public humiliation. In an interview with *Modern Rock Live*, Fred outlined the scenario that ended with him naked on stage. "I played naked in France because Jonathan and his Korn dogs decided to give me five hundred dollars to do it and I did it because I was broke. . . . I needed money so they said five hundred bucks if I got naked and sang 'Faith,' and it was pretty embarassing because my little bobo had shriveled up into negative form and sucked up into my body. This was where the helmet took a dive ya know, when I was on the stage in front of thousands of people."

After landing back in Florida with the Warped dates wrapped and the foray across European soil a done deal, Fred got a call from Les Claypool of Primus, inviting Limp Bizkit to join Primus on a fall tour before their eclectic crowds. Wes, a fan of Primus since age fourteen, said to the web site Spinal Column that he was thrilled at the prospect of touring with Primus, but also concerned that their remarkably devoted fan base might not be open to a new act. "Les Claypool called Fred's house and talked to Fred for a while. He really wanted us to do it, because we were a little sketchy about it at first. We're thinking Faith No More's crowd's a little weird, Primus's crowd is a lot weirder. I've been into Primus for a long time, and they've always been one of my favorite bands. So hopefully there's some people like me, who are into what we're doing as well."

Les Claypool said Limp Bizkit's stint as openers for Primus opened his eyes at the time, but that even though he thought they would do well, he never anticipated the extent of the success they would later have. "Limp Bizkit was one of those bands, every now and then a band opened for you and you step back and say 'Whoa, these guys are pretty damn good.' I always expected they would do well but I don't think anybody expected them to do as well as they're doing. Nobody expects anybody to do that well. Fred's a salesman, he's good at pushing that product. I know those guys take a lot of knocks for being so popular. I'm the first one to sit back and look at things that are oversaturated and start backing away from it, but watching them even then, they were a really good live band."

Before a show at Iowa State University, Wes told the campus rag that the tour was going swimmingly with Limp Bizkit taking the Primus trademark of getting fans to chant "Primus Sucks," and giving it their own Big Freddie style twist, with band members taking the stage with middle fingers aloft. "They finger us back—and you know what that means to us—that they love us. It's kind of like saying something is bad when you really mean good. Les Claypool came out the first night of the tour and got a big kick out of it," Wes said in an interview. "We figured it was the right idea. It makes hecklers go 'huh.' "

As a means of beating the monotony of the road, Wes developed a patented prank that's fun for everybody but the person who discovers it long after he's gone. In an interview in the October 1997 issue of *Guitar World*, Wes sketched out his scheme. "When we're backstage, I pop out a ceiling tile and put an open milk carton up there, then put the tile back. No one knows it's there until it starts to stink and then when they push the ceiling tile up to find out what's causing the smell, the milk spills all over them."

If a prank isn't the answer to break up the monotony, Wes turns to deadpan and deceit to avoid having to pontificate on what Limp Bizkit's metal and rap marriage sounds like to the uninitiated. "If I'm having a real bad day, and I don't feel like explaining it, I just say, 'You wouldn't like it. It really sucks,' " Wes told *Guitar World*. "If somebody asks us if we're in a band at truck stops, we always say we're a traveling soccer team or we're with the circus."

After finishing yet another outing, this time with the Deftones, Fred and DJ Lethal got tapped by Max Cavalera of Soulfly to make a guest appearance on Soulfly's debut LP. Formed after a difficult split from Sepultura, the Brazilian heavy metal act fronted by Cavalera for over a decade, Cavalera said Durst was recommended for a guest spot by Robinson, at a time when Limp Bizkit was still unknown. "When we were in the studio doing the Soulfly album, the idea was to collaborate with a lot of people and make it like a rap type of ideology with people dropping in on every song. Chino from the Deftones was one of them and Fred was one of them. . . . I had this killer song 'Bleed' . . . Fred met with me and I was like this is some serious heavy shit. It's about my really close friend being murdered. I'd like you to rap on it but keep the spirit. I left the vocal booth and Ross said walk around and let us do our thing and then come back and listen. I stayed outside the studio for about two hours and when I came back it was awesome. Fred's part was really cool. I shook his hand and told him it was awesome and thanks for doing this. I really love how it turned out."

Fred's vocals also surfaced on Korn's "Follow the Leader," on the decidedly less emotionally wrenching "All in the Family." Korn singer Jonathan Davis told the *Minneapolis Star-Tribune* that the vicious banter between him and Fred in the tune sometimes leads people to believe the two bands don't get along. "It's just me and him ragging on each other. Some kids think that Korn and Limp Bizkit hate each other. But hey, why we would be in the same room talking to each other if we hated each other? We have total respect. Originally, the song was for B Real of Cypress Hill. But his record label wouldn't let him do it. I'm glad, because this came out way better."

Rather than ad-lib the track the way some of Fred's favorite MCs might have before the Old School let out, Davis told Addicted To Noise that he and Fred wrote out their rapped insults ahead of time, calling each other on the phone to give updates, with each being impressed by the other's derisive skills. "We wrote it all out. I'm not fuckin' Mr. Freestyle like Fred is, so I went back and wrote some stuff. It came off really good. We were just like, 'Let's bag on each other and make kids freak out and call each other up on the phone, and say, "Ah, fuck—did you hear that shit?" ' "

While the teasing was meant in good fun, Jon admitted in an interview with earwig.com that there were times when both he and Fred took the potshots seriously. "After we recorded the album we played a show with Limp Bizkit and I saw Fred. And I said, 'Fucker, why did you have to say this and that? Why did you have to bag on me about my teeth?' " Still Jon acknowledged in the same interview that during the writing of the song, it was him riding Fred to up the ante. "He would throw a bag at me, and I would help him out. He was like, 'Tootin' on your bagpipe' and I would say, 'Why don't you say 'Tooting on your fagpipes?' I helped him bag on me better."

On a rare break from touring, Wes married his fiancée Heather MacMillan on April 10, 1998 and then embarked on a brief honeymoon punctuated by stops at amusement parks in each of the towns on their itinerary. Limp Bizkit dutifully ended Web's bachelor days with a party that sent him wobbling into married life. "As soon as I walked in the door, there were ten guys standing all around me, each holding up a different bottle of hard liquor," remembered Wes in an article in the CMJ *New Music Monthly*. "I'd open my eyes and there'd be Captain Morgan's or Goldschläger in front of me. They found the worst strippers . . . I don't know if they should even be called women. They got naked and were covered with scars and hair in bad places, and they tried to get me to start doing stuff with them. . . . Thank God that, because of the shots, I had to vomit immediately."

Building on the initial friendship with Fred, Soulfly picked Limp Bizkit as openers for their European tour in early 1998. In turn, Fred's first pet project, Cold, tagged along with Limp Bizkit, the way Limp Bizkit followed in Korn's footsteps a little earlier. Max said that Limp Bizkit's determination impressed him, given the fact that they were playing to audiences that were largely unfamiliar with their music. "I don't know if I thought they'd be as big a band as they'd become, but they had a lot of hunger. They were serious about what they were doing. The music with the hip-hop had a different aspect that could reach a lot of people. I saw that potential back in the days when I saw Soundgarden. I thought, 'This is a really killer band. I think this band is going to be big.'"

With Limp Bizkit along, Soulfly took advantage of Fred's presence and brought him out onstage each night to sing "Bleed." Providing Soulfly with the personnel that appeared on the record and Limp Bizkit with a shot of cred in the arm from an established musical force worked well for both bands. "Fred used to come out to sing 'Bleed' with us wearing only a sock, a fucked-up looking sock that you could see through. I got tripped out sometimes and I'd be like 'Man, you're scaring me right now' but it was cool. He came to sing 'Bleed' with us every night and it was always awesome."

Along the way, Limp Bizkit began developing a live show, that Fred says gets so intense as to cause bodily harm to members of the band. At one Atlanta show, Fred managed to injure himself. "We didn't realize how hard it is to tour—especially when you're a band like us," Fred told the *Alternative Press*. "We go off hard—our stage show, I think, is one of the top ten in the world. But when you go off that hard and it's that good of a show, it's unpredictable. We were halfway through our set; my abdominal area was hurting, and in the middle of our song 'Stuck' I buckled over and passed out."

Touring consistently paid off in a big way for Limp Bizkit. With the band resting up after nearly an entire year on the road, "Faith" began justifying the belief that Jordan Schur had in Limp Bizkit when he first signed them to a record deal. "We released 'Faith' as soon as we stopped touring, and 'Faith' took off during our off-time," Wes told the *Denver Rocky Mountain News*. "We grew more than we ever had from touring. It was just like the biggest blessing."

Limp Bizkit is quick to point out that *Three Dollar Bill Y'all* went gold before "Faith" broke into the mainstream. Their cover of George Michael's 80s standard functioned as a porthole that allowed Limp Bizkit to creep onto the radio, according to Jim Kerr, alternative editor at the industry trade magazine *Radio & Records*. " 'Faith' opened a lot of radio doors and that's a very important thing. In that particular time period, alternative radio was still playing Cherry Poppin' Daddies and Big Bad Voodoo Daddy. Going from swing to "Nookie" is not something that could happen overnight. 'Faith' gave radio a comfortable song from a band that radio knew had a grassroots following and could be potentially huge. It's like the first date thing, we'll give it a shot here. I'll take you to the dance as long as you behave. Of course now they're home alone in a dark room."

With "Faith" starting to make waves, winning a slot on the Ozzfest provided Limp Bizkit the ideal forum to play to fans who were beginning to know who they were. Prior to hitting the road for Ozzfest, Limp Bizkit sat down with MTV and Fred explained the unifying factor of a bill that included such acts as the Melvins, Tool, Soulfly, and the Ozzman himself. "All these bands really have a very strong drive to them and a very emotional side that comes out with some heavy guitars, you know. Just that darker side of music . . . I think we're all a little bit on the darker side of life you know, that everything's not daisies and sunshine, it's . . . its's Ozzfest in sunshine."

Cavalera said his band and Limp Bizkit paled around at the Ozzfest, having barbecues and checking up on each other every now and then. "When you know a band from touring together before, it tends to be like a friendship. They'd come by and say, 'What's up, man?' and we'd end up hanging out. Apart from them, a lot of the other bands on the Ozzfest we didn't know much about. They were the band we knew, apart from Ozzy and we knew him more from the past."

Even after a nearly constant touring schedule, Limp Bizkit still endured the heckling of fans unconvinced by their hybrid of rap and metal, with detractors harping on the misogynistic tone of Fred's lyrics or their uninspired name. In response to the criticism, Limp Bizkit emerged from a thirty-foot toilet each night on the Ozzfest and punctuated their sets by flushing cardboard cutouts of the band's sworn enemies such as Hanson and the Spice Girls onstage.

Fred reflected on the decision to rise like feces out of the W.C. as yet another stunt necessary to help Limp Bizkit achieve their long-term goals, in an interview with *Rolling Stone*. "Everybody was saying 'Limp Bizkit is shit.' So we said, 'Okay, we'll be shit. We'll make a gigantic toilet and come out of it like five turds.' We got their attention. They were watchin' the show, and they were buyin' the records. You gotta do that sometimes, man."

Although the oversize toilet was all Limp Bizkit's doing, Snot singer Lynn Strait made headlines July 9, 1998, at Great Woods in Mansfield, Massachusetts, by emerging from the toilet, wearing nothing more than a cocky grin. Max said Strait's stunt was a source of great amusement to all the bands on the tour and made his death in a car accident less than six months later all the more poignant.

All nudity aside, responsive crowds delighted in the toilet humor and reacted so enthusiastically that festival organizers began to have second thoughts about keeping Limp Bizkit in the lineup. Wes said the rowdy ruffians' behavior made Sharon Osbourne, Ozzy's wife and manager, more than a little upset with Limp Bizkit. "The Ozzfest has seats, and we almost got kicked off the first two days of the tour for getting the kids to break through the barricades," Wes said in an interview with *Guitar World*. "Sharon Osbourne was pretty angry with us because we almost incited riots."

Part of the excitement of Ozzfest for Limp Bizkit was the chance to tour with and watch Tool play each night. Members of Limp Bizkit routinely proclaim to interviewers that Tool makes music that must be the product of pacts similar to the one that bluesman Robert Johnson made with the devil at the crossroads, just as Fred did in talking to MTV. "Tool is like one of my favorite bands. I mean, they are beyond a doubt one of the best bands in the world. Whether you like them or not, you just can't help but respect what they're doing. It's phenomenal. They take you on a journey with every song, and it seems like it's perfect, you know? I really believe that when he says he sold his soul to make a record."

As star of the show, Ozzy was free to make his own arrangements for travel. In an interview with MTV News in the early days of the Ozzfest, Wes suggested what he believed to be Ozzy's MO for getting to shows. "Actually, he's teleported in by way of the cashmere effect. Two platelets will be in London, and there are two platelets that are on that big red bus over there. And what happens is they send them through one side and automatically a small wormhole is created, and Ozzy automatically appears, BAM, right here at the Ozzfest."

Although Ozzy rarely, if ever, arrived at Ozzfest shows in the manner Wes described, he did come away from his self-designed package tour impressed by Limp Bizkit. In an interview with the web site Addicted To Noise in August of 1998, he explained how the Ozzfest came to be and fingered Limp Bizkit as his favorite new act on the tour. "The concept came from being fed up with doing an album, touring, doing an album, touring," he said. "All of a sudden, the musical format changed and there was no outlet for these bands. I thought, that's wrong. MTV shouldn't be the ones that govern what's on the air. A lot of these young bands don't have outlets to play. So I said, 'Fuck it, I'll do my own thing,'" said Ozzy, adding his plug for his favorite newcomer. "Limp Bizkit are fucking brilliant," he said. "They're going to be really good, no doubt about it."

Drummer John Otto suffered the lone setback in what was an otherwise successful Ozzfest stint, after spending a night in the slammer in Auburn Hills, Michigan, on a misdemeanor charge of carrying a concealed weapon. "He allegedly fired a BB gun, and investigating officers found him to be carrying a switchblade," said Lt. David Chase of the Auburn Hills police to the web site Addicted To Noise. "He spent the night in jail and was released the next morning. He plead guilty and was fined two thousand dollars." In retrospect Otto was able to laugh about his overnighter in the pokey, in an article that ran in *Spin*. "He was cool about it. He said, 'If you were the drummer from Def Leppard, it would have been all right,' " said Otto of the arresting officer.

When the final numbers were counted, the Ozzfest was one of the top grossing tours of 1998. Getting a boost in profile for Limp Bizkit was important but what was becoming increasingly apparent and important was that there was a great demand for bands that represented the heavier end of music. Known music industry analyst Ozzy Osbourne told CNN that he couldn't really explain why the metal aspect of music was popular, but he wasn't exactly going looking for answers either. "I have no idea why we did so well. But I don't even try and understand. Perhaps it's because we're not pretentious—we don't try to be what we're not. We do what we do, we do it well, and we're low-key about it. So we never built ourselves up to be let down. Festivals like Ozzfest fill a need for a certain genre of music. Lilith Fair is fantastic and nothing competes with it. The same goes for us."

Ozzfest completed, Limp Bizkit took a breather to rest up for Korn's Family Values Tour, storing the thirty-foot toilet in a Jacksonville ministorage unit and brainstorming ideas for a new stage set to accompany their live act. Titled "Family Values" as an ironic jab at the GOP campaign slogan years earlier, Korn singer Jonathan Davis told *Rolling Stone* that rankling those who coined the term was only part of the fun. "We're asking for trouble. Politicians say rock music is destroying our youth. We named it 'Family Values' to piss those people off. It's going to be a parents-free zone."

Putting together a festival tour that included themselves and other like-minded bands had long been on the Korn agenda, Fieldy asserted to the Addicted To Noise web site, but with rock bands' hectic schedules being what they are it wasn't until the fall of 1998 that all the pieces of the package-puzzle fell into place. "We've been trying to get it together forever. We just haven't had the right bands. Or we had one of the right bands, not enough for a festival. The ones that we wanted to take out were either busy working on albums or already on another tour. But now we've got all the bands together, and it's so good."

With a lineup assembled by Limp Bizkit bene-factors Korn, the Family Values roster shared the same basic sensibilities and styles, which Korn guitarist Brian "Head" Welch told the *Houston Press* was the whole idea. "We just kind of threw it together. We wanted to take [Limp] Bizkit because they're a good live band, and they are friends of ours. It was about having fun, mainly, for us, and giving the crowd a good variety of music that would blend in together. Ice Cube, we've been fans of his forever. . . . Orgy is on our new label and they are friends of ours too, so we brought them."

Bringing arena rock back is a tall order. With kids accustomed to near constant entertainment, through TV, movies, the Internet, and video games, it takes a lot more to pack the house than swabbing on a little face paint or detonating some run of the mill explosives. Korn and Limp Bizkit manager Jeff Kwatinetz pointed out to wallofsound.com that developing an exciting show production ranked nearly on a par with picking a red-hot lineup. "We know that kids love going to arena shows," said Kwantinetz. "It's not just a matter of talent, but of production. We don't want kids going home and saying, 'Yeah, it was good.' We want them going home and calling ten of their friends and say, 'It was incredible. I saw God.'"

The *L.A. Times* described Limp Bizkit's Family Values stage set as a mix of *The War of the Worlds* and *Mars Attacks*, and noted the band's entrance from a spaceship and the performance of a cadre of break-dancers as elements that enhanced the live show. In addition to the extensive stage productions, Wes continued to make himself a one-man art project each night, delving into his art-school background to give himself a slightly different freakish image each night. "We don't really put on an act onstage," Wes told the *Baltimore Sun*. "I mean, I wear some really crazy [stuff] onstage, because I'm a visual artist, too, and I really have a problem with going onstage just looking like myself. I think it's boring. I'd rather wear a funny suit and paint my face yellow and have big black contact lenses."

After the Ozzfest, where Ozzy was the undisputed focal point of the tour, Fred told MTV that the Family Values tour was a little more of an egalitarian affair, with elaborate stage sets for each act the norm. "[Ozzy] was the star of the show. This one it's Korn's Family Values Tour, but it's like, everyone has full use of the stage. There's nothing up on the stage but your production. And it's gigantic. Everyone has a huge production. It's like pretty unheard of. This is the first time in our generation for this to be happening to us. It's like a Macy's Day Parade and every float is phatter than the next."

Korn singer Jonathan Davis offered the web site Wall of Sound a rundown on Family Values' phat floats, a collection of unique efforts with a unifying theme of bright lights and fire. "Everyone's production is insane," Davis says. "Rammstein's got a zillion white lights and all this fire, pyrotechnic shit. Ice Cube has got a big, giant bust of himself, it's like thirty feet high and says 'Ice Cube the Great.' . . . Limp Bizkit has a giant UFO that's crashed, which is gonna be killer, and Orgy's full-on; they said it looks like *Rollerball*, but it's big, giant white squares over their amps, with some blue lights in 'em. It's very futuristic."

The camaraderie between the bands on the

Family Values tour made possible shows like the Halloween gig at the Patriot Center in Fairfax, Virginia, where each of the acts offered up a trick or treat for the appreciative audience. Fairfax's finest didn't respond well to the fire-loving Rammstein's choice to play mostly naked, shutting them down after about ten minutes. But the fuzz didn't see fit to halt Limp Bizkit's set, when each of the members came out dressed as Elvis at different stages in his career. And John Q. Law didn't have a problem with Korn's choice to come out dressed like a hair-metal band and cover songs such as the Scorpion's "Rock You Like A Hurricane," or Twisted Sister's "We're Not Gonna Take It."

When it came time to shoot a video for "Faith," Fred wanted his direction to reflect what a band living their dream looked like. Playing to audiences familiar with their music was making a drastic difference and even if most of the kids could only thrash along with "Faith," Limp Bizkit now had at least one song they knew would get the kids standing and screaming along. In an interview with MTV during the Family Values tour, Fred explained his vision for the video, that reflected Limp Bizkit's rejuvenated live show. "Right now, what's going on with Family Values is the best time of our life and it's the most fun, anticipated tour that anyone could possibly . . . you gotta go to it. And it's like we had to capture it, from waking up in the morning, to backstage, to setting up, to playing live to the thousands and thousands of people, the energy, the stage props, the people on tour . . . Ice Cube, Korn, everybody's in the video."

The original version of the "Faith" video was shot in Hollywood's Key Club. Limp Bizkit invited fans to be the audience for the shoot and VIPs such as Korn and Incubus looked on. The band warmed up with House of Pain staple "Jump Around," and their own "Counterfeit." Fred wore a black T-shirt and led a crowd that moshed around "like buffalos with epilepsy" as described by addictedtonoise.com's Teri vanHorn.

Once the buffalos shuffled off, Limp Bizkit decided the Key Club version of "Faith" didn't quite match their idea of what the band was about and the new version with the Family Values footage was commissioned. Wes explained the band's decision to the *Denver Rocky Mountain News.* "It was just really not a good video. It wasn't his fault. It would have been a good video for another band, but for us it was not a good thing. We shot another one over the course of three or four days—just us playing and being stupid. It was shot very inexpensively. The other video was a huge, expensive production that the film and record company was behind. But this one had more heart."

Interscope president Tom Whalley said that during the second take of the "Faith" video, he saw a new facet of Fred, the perfectionist that dreams of being "Freddie Ford Coppola," a megamedia mogul and not merely a musician. "I didn't really see that incredibly ambitious side of him until he made that video," said Whalley in an interview with *Spin*. "We had made one version in conjunction with the movie *Very Bad Things*, and it didn't turn out that great. Fred called me up and begged me to let him do it again. It turned out to be a crowning moment for him."

In keeping with the feel of "Indigo Flow," in the second take, Limp Bizkit used the "Faith" video as a thank you to bands such as Primus and the Deftones that brought them out on early tours where audiences knew them only as that opening band with the funny name. Shot in slow motion, in the same manner that Motley Crüe's "Home Sweet Home" video once was, Fred included behind the scenes bits he was convinced fans wanted to see. "Tommy Lee's in the video, from Mötley Crüe, you know Chino from the Deftones, Les Claypool from Primus, everybody's in this video," Fred said to MTV. "All the backstage, everything. You want to see what goes on on-tour, we're letting you see it. We're bringing it to you, and somebody hasn't done that in a while, or really hasn't captured it, so we figured this song George Michael has created for us is the perfect time to release what's going on on-tour."

While the kids felt much love for Limp Bizkit's super-charged cover of "Faith," one person who wasn't rushing to the Best Buy to pick up a copy was George Michael. Wes told Addicted To Noise that the band heard through reliable sources that not only does Michael not like the new version, he hates it. "What we've heard from George Michael's people is that he hates it and hates us for doing it," Wes said. "He apparently really despises it."

Strangely, outside of George Michael's displeasure with Limp Bizkit's "Faith," the band took the most heat for its success from the fans themselves. In Internet chatrooms and on Limp Bizkit web sites the clamor of criticism accusing Limp Bizkit of selling out grew to such a level that Wes responded to the indignant teens, in a posting in all caps on Dike 99's web site, where he offered no apologies for their recent success. "Three years before MTV gave us any kind of notice at all, I ate, drank, slept, and lived filth for three years on tour, made almost no money at all, almost never was at home, grew apart from my family and friends, and gave up everything for this band. We made it now. I'm thrilled that we are on MTV."

# Four

The recording of *Significant Other* couldn't have started at a better time. Riding the crest of the breakout success of "Faith," the band was eager to get in the studio and show they weren't a flukey cover act or Korn, Jr. In an interview with *Guitar World*, Wes said Limp Bizkit's tutelage under Bakersfield's best sometimes was a double-edged sword. "Too many people started calling us Baby Korn. Korn showed us the ropes of touring but I don't think we've taken anything musically from them. Anyway, it's time to leave the mother's nest." Recording an album that could make people think of Limp Bizkit apart from Korn or George Michael provided ample motivation to record. Fred's personal struggles were also giving him more inspiration than he knew what to do with.

The uncertainty of fame hardly qualifies as anything new, but as *Three Dollar Bill Y'all* continued to make Limp Bizkit into the rock stars they'd dreamed of, Fred found himself doubting the sincerity of some of his friends and his girlfriend in particular. As he told *Billboard* online, Limp Bizkit was beginning to write a record that would address the year plus of touring and adjusting to life as rock stars. "I learned a lot from touring, and I've made wrong decisions in terms of business partners and girlfriends. I want to thank all the people who betrayed me, because they gave me the emotions that are on this album. [*Significant Other*] is a big 'thank you' to them."

Fred learned that while he and the rest of Limp Bizkit spent their days and nights trying to establish a rapport with new audiences, his girlfriend was not sitting at home and pining away for his return from tour, but was establishing a very intimate rapport with some new audiences of her own. Fred's well-documented frustrations with his ex-girlfriend provided excellent angst-ridden material for the new record, spawning tracks such as "Nookie" and "Rearranged" that directly addressed his anger and sadness at staying so long with a girl that treated him so bad. Like a chump as he might say, he stuck around long after he should have walked away. As Fred's inadvertent muse, she helped spark songs that got the kids in the backward caps and the Kangol hats pumping their fists with righteous indignation at her wayward ways.

"It was one of these relationships where I was

on tour, and she's sleeping with my friends. I'm sending her a gang of money, I'm supporting her, and she'd say, 'Oh, I lost the money.' Or 'I need more money,' " Fred told *Guitar* magazine in their August 1999 issue. "She was just using me so bad. I would find out things, little things, and I would keep forgiving her. Because I had been with her for so long, like three and a half years."

Added incentive to write a new record came from the fact that during their incessant touring for *Three Dollar Bill Y'all* Limp Bizkit only had one album's worth of material to pull from, making for some pretty similar set lists. While fans fretted as bandwagon types hopped on after the success of "Faith," Limp Bizkit was itching to write some new songs, every bit as much as the fans were wanting to hear them. In a posting on Dike 99's Limp Bizkit web site, Wes said in no uncertain terms that he welcomed the opportunity to write some new tunes. "If teeny bopper 'Faith' nerds piss you off, ignore them. Honestly, I'm totally sick of 'Faith' too, along with all of our old shit. I don't care if I never hear it or have to play it again! I hate *Three Dollar Bill* now."

The phenomenon of a band sitting in a studio and writing songs for a record shouldn't be a particularly revolutionary concept but as the Britney Spears and Christina Aguileras of the music world maintain a stranglehold on MTV's *TRL* and the top of the charts, Limp Bizkit's ability to write records and sell them in healthy quantity almost qualifies as a rarity. In an interview with launch.com, Wes said Limp Bizkit takes particular pride in their songwriting because it sets them apart from other teenscream acts that sell records in the same numbers that McDonalds sells burgers, without being able to play a note of music themselves. "We are a five-member rock band, and we write as a rock band and don't let anyone else tell us what to do. A lot of these other groups, the pop bands and the boy bands and the fifteen-year-old Britney Spears pop star people are just pretty much put together by other groups."

With a platinum record to their credit, Limp Bizkit could set their own timetable for the writing of the new album. Early on, the band needed to get a record written to have something to sell to fans at shows. "Counterfeit" bought them extra time and Wes told *Maximum Guitar* they wanted to take full advantage of it. "Our last record, seventy percent of it was written in six days. It's pretty easy for us to write when we can close out the outside world. I think the new record will be a new level for us. The stuff we've written for it so far has been pretty experimental—definitely a step up from the old record. We're playing around with different timings, out of the four/four groove thing, doing a couple of rhythms in seven."

Fred's rocky love life, while good fodder for lyrics, can't carry the band on its own. Part of what fuels Limp Bizkit is the disparity between the band's two poles, Fred and Wes. As much as Wes loves to dress up in costumes onstage and look like someone that's not of this earth, Fred revels in thinking of himself as only a couple million dollars and a few years removed from the fans that pack Limp Bizkit's shows. And where Wes might think of Ween's *The Mollusk* as perfect road music, Fred's discman would be much more likely to have Pearl Jam's *Ten* spinning around in it than anything that eclectic.

In an interview with *Guitar World* Wes admitted that the band does battle over which direction the songwriting should go, but points out that this intensity and conflict benefits the music. "We don't use anything that all of us aren't excited by. If we do something and one person doesn't get goosebumps, we don't use it. Like, if John says, 'I really don't like that part,' we'll go. 'It's gone.' Maybe it will feel different later, or something like that. But if we're not happy with something we'll throw it out."

Part of the tensions stemmed from the fears Limp Bizkit felt at taking their music in a new direction. Finding different ways to express themselves caused the band to feel uncertain and doubt each other's opinions about the new songs. "It was real uncomfortable during the process," Wes told the *Denver Rocky Mountain News*. "We were really unsure and arguing a lot and we were getting upset a lot. A lot of what we wanted to do was scaring us so much. For me, approaching melody and getting away from hiding behind effects pedals, . . . that was a big thing for me. We said, 'Let's do something meaty instead of some sort of tofu guitar line and spice it up with effects.' "

The years spent touring paid off as the Limp lads began writing songs for the new record. Following each other's leads and covering each other's mistakes night after night before a live audience helped the ability to anticipate how different members react to different situations. All of which made the writing of the second record easier than the first. "That's kind of what happened; we all understand each other more now," Wes said to launch.com. "After playing together for a really long time, we're all able to predict what the other ones are going to do so we can write parts that complement the other people's parts."

This increased awareness of each other's musical tendencies manifested itself on *Significant Other* in the writing of "Don't Go Off Wandering," that began with Wes's homegrown guitar parts and grew into a fully fleshed-out song as each of the band members offered their ideas to add on to his skeletal construct. " 'Don't Go Off Wandering' was three guitar parts that I wrote at home and recorded on a four-track, using an acoustic guitar," Wes informed *Guitar World*. "Everybody went, 'Oh shit, that's really cool.' So Sam made up a bass line that changed it a little bit, and then Fred said, 'What if you take this guitar part and take out a couple notes, so it's just like these four flowing notes?' And I was, like, 'Oh, yeah. That works pretty good.' "

Up until the writing of *Significant Other*, DJ Lethal's role consisted primarily of adding subtle touches to tracks written by Wes, John, and Sam but when Method Man expressed interest in making a guest appearance on the album, the band stepped back and let Lethal loose. "Lee had been programming and making a lot of beats and a lot of hip-hop stuff, and he and Fred had wanted to get down and do some nitty-gritty MC/DJ stuff to really get into our hip-hop roots. So we wanted a track that was straight hip-hop," Wes explained to *Guitar One*. "And we all look up to the Wu-Tang Clan and Method Man so much; it was just such an honor to have him on the record."

Along with the initial ideas for "N 2 Gether," the parts DJ Lethal wrote for the new record helped flesh out Limp Bizkit's sound, adding textures without disrupting the flow of the song. "If you hear any long, droned-out sounds that you can't match with an instrument, that's me. That's the role that I present," Lethal said in an interview with *Smug*. "That's the way I like to do it. I'll make enough noise to let you know I'm here, but I'll keep you guessing about how much of myself I'm holding back."

Abandoning his usual diplomatic posture, Wes confirmed in an interview with launch.com, that the girl who teased and tortured Fred with her exploits while he was on tour is every bit the heartbreaker, love taker, Fred says she is. "It's really amazing how horrible this girl is. I don't want to say 'Oh, no, it's not as bad as you think'; it is. I feel sorry for her 'cause she's got some major mental problems, and she's really just gonna be in for a life of suffering and pain and guilt if she continues to live that way or continues to show the behavior that she did when she was with him."

The girl in question helped spark "Nookie," Fred's anthem for everyone who's ever spent too much time in a bad relationship, for the basest of reasons. The aggressive venting of "Break Stuff" sidesteps the comparatively more artistic lyrical approach that Fred opted for with "Nookie" and cuts straight to the angry chase. "Everybody's had one of those days where you're just like, 'Leave me alone. Don't talk to me. Just keep your distance, man.' You know what I mean? I was having that day when I wrote it," Fred said in the August 1999 issue of *Guitar World*. "The song was poppin'. After I got done, I was like, 'Man, the promoter's liability on this song . . .' I don't think it's going to make a crowd hurt each other. I think it's just going to be that little feather on the camel's back, that one little push that turns it into, 'Wow, things are really intense now.'"

Again, Fred emphasized the importance of keeping the lyrics as accessible as a 7-11 and took a swipe at fellow Floridians Matchbox 20 while he was at it. "I swing it a couple different ways on the new record but I'm talking about common things," said Fred to the CMJ's *New Music Monthly*. "It's straightforward. Matchbox 20's songs are huge, but when you sing about, 'It's three A.M. and I'm in a coffee shop . . .' how many people are really going to get into that?"

In addition to the usual challenges a band faces in writing good songs for a record, Limp Bizkit knew that pressure and expectations were being placed on them by fans and Interscope because of the success of *Three Dollar Bill Y'all*. Wes reflected on the differences in writing the two records in an interview with launch.com. "There's no comparison between the two records, as far as I'm concerned. *Three Dollar Bill* was an easy record to write 'cause we were not thinking. We had nothing to live up to. We were brand new, we had just gotten signed, there was a super high level of excitement. And it's really easy to write real heavy tunes, no matter what anybody says. It's a lot harder to write music and to get more melodic and try to actually have songs within those heavy, droning, angstful power chords."

In an interview with hiponline.com, bassist Sam Rivers seconded Wes's point, observing that with the first record the band was like a jittery debutante, just happy to get invited to the big dance, and with the second they were more inclined to take their time like true divas, primping and preening until they got their sound just right. "The first record, we were young and we were just glad to be doing a record. It was like a dream come true, but it was really rushed, not in a bad way, just everything was real quick. And this record was a product of two years on the road and learning what works and what doesn't."

Rather than throw together a rash of big-selling singles Wes told *Smug* magazine that Limp Bizkit began writing *Significant Other* with their favorite albums, such as Tool's *Aenima* and Nirvana's *Nevermind* on the brain, records that function as a whole and not as future fodder for a "Hits of '99" compilation. "People stopped looking at records as whole [albums]—and that's fine. But we try and get [the songs] to flow into each other and look at the record as a song. That's really important. That's what the greats in the past did. [Albums] aren't meant to have a message, just look at it as one piece."

With little free time to write new songs, Wes said the band tries to make the best use possible out of the slender time slots afforded them during tours. "We jam all the time. We use our sound-checks to have band practice on tour, basically . . ." he said in a profile by launch.com. "Instead of sound-checking normal songs, we're having band practice and writing." One song that originated in this manner is "Re-arranged," which came together in rough form in early 1998, during the Ladies Night in Cambodia tour and later was polished in the pre-production stages of *Significant Other*. "I'm Broke" also kicked around for a couple years, missing the cut for *Three Dollar Bill Y'all* when it didn't quite mesh with the other tracks, while the single "Nookie" turned out to be an eleventh hour addition.

"I'm Broke" was recorded for *Three Dollar Bill* and never made it on the record because it was different; it didn't have a lot of the same parts and was redone," Wes explained to launch.com. "But a lot of stuff was written right at the record; 'Nookie' was written during recording. It was the last song written for the record, after preproduction, one day out of nowhere. It's pretty cool for that to be the one that ended up being a single and hitting really big."

With the writing of *Significant Other*, the effects of touring constantly and spending nearly every moment of every day with each other for four years began to surface in Limp Bizkit's songwriting. Knowing each other much better musically and personally helped corral even as elusive an art as songwriting into a more orderly process. "Fred is an amazing arranger, and basically we know what he's going to do lyric-wise, and so we know how to write for him, how to write a part that he can write lyrics to. Sometimes he'll write [lyrics] while we're writing the songs," Wes said to launch.com. "He'll have an old set of lyrics he wrote some time ago and he'll sing 'em in place of something, or sometimes he just will be improvising or he'll start freestyling, and that will become the song."

Fred lists keeping his angst readily comprehensible and accessible as a priority for himself as a lyricist, in particular as he was writing the words for *Significant Other*, fearing that if he dug too deep into his artistic trough, he could wind up alienating the very fan base that the crunching power chords and the sly break-beats of their music was attempting to entice. Fred outlined his quality control standards for his lyrics in an interview with *New Music Monthly*, "What are you going to write about? Is this song saying something that most everybody is going to feel, that they'll comprehend and get? Is it a feeling that's common in ninety percent of all human beings? I don't go on these eclectic whims, and beat around the bush with terminology that people won't get."

Beyond keeping it accessible, the hailstorm of criticism accusing Fred of writing misogynistic lyrics caused him to exert some amount of caution in how he phrased his rants. "I was angry at my girlfriend and I let it build up," Fred told *Rolling Stone*. "If you heard what she called me . . . I understand that two wrongs don't make a right. I was reacting; I didn't think of the consequences. Now I soak everything in and then I respond. And when someone criticizes my lyrics it makes me think twice." This kind of self-censorship manifests itself most

*Robyn Heller*

*Robyn Heller*

*Robyn Heller*

*Robyn Heller*

*Robyn Heller*

*Jen Lowery*

*Robyn Heller*

*Jen Lowery*

obviously in "Nookie," where Fred suggests that someone take that cookie and stick it up their "yeah," when a lot of other words seem to fit more easily into that slot.

Much of the flak directed at Fred centered around the lyrics to "Stuck." Screaming bitch and whore in a tone that suggests the singer might be wearing a wife-beater and bellowing for a potpie, angered the politically correct and concerned. In conversation with the *NME*, Fred acknowledged his caustic word choice but insisted that he was merely accurately describing a former girlfriend. "Well I use the words 'bitch' and 'whore' in the song, directed towards one person who was both of those things, if you ask me. To the naked eye, people that didn't want to take the time and listen to the words, might think otherwise. But I definitely respect women. I have a better attitude than almost anyone I know towards women." Fred further defended his lyrics to the *Washington Post*, by saying that Limp Bizkit's female fans outnumber the males and that the women hear something in his words that the testostoroned types miss. "I'm a heterosexual man that sings about the emotional stress and pain I've had from love and realities of intimacy. The pain and anger that I feel about love that I've experienced is about women. Somebody may hear the word 'bitch' in our songs, but I love women. I will always be ready for my soulmate to fall into my lap. So those people who think it's derogatory towards women are the people that aren't listening to the words."

Fred's mother Anita, while acknowledging that she's not a fan of the swearing that punctuates many of Limp Bizkit's songs, informed the *NME* that as an adult, Fred's entitled to his creative license in the Durst home. "Well I'm a mother so I don't care for the cursing, but Fred expresses himself. He's twenty-nine years old, you know? Fred does what he does creatively and I approve of everything Fred does. You know what it is? Fred loves being him and I love being Fred's Mom!"

Without much of the fury from *Three Dollar Bill Y'all*, and with an endorsement from his mom, Fred described the new batch of tunes to allmusic.com as more mature and attributed this to his adoption of a more adult way of handling the problems in his life. "The record's about being abused, but it's about accepting that this has happened to you. It's about why I put up with it and why it happened to me. I guess I'm angry, but I accept why things have happened. The first record was more like I'm really angry and I'm attacking the source that made me feel like this. Now I'm angry, but it's a little more controlled, a little more thought-out and mature."

Fred attributed the more polished feel of the new batch of Bizkit songs to a desire to show the distance Limp Bizkit had covered since the recording of their first record in the waning days of 1996 at Ross Robinson's Indigo Ranch. "If I made the same record again, what would that show my fans? What was I doing for two and a half years? Sitting around with my thumb up my ass? Getting angry got me nowhere," Fred said to CMJ's *New Music Monthly.* "So on this record, I'm at the next level. And by the next record, who knows how I'm going to deal with anything in my life. But as time goes, fans go and bands go. They grow, we grow."

Perhaps part of the mature bent Fred talked of, "No Sex" shaped up lyrically as an abstinence anthem, with Fred shunning the more accepted rockstar posture of the more sex the better, for a safer and less interesting stance. "I've been in a position where you don't ever want to talk to that person again, no matter how fine they are. It's just like a waste. There's no bond, no great friendship, and all that's left is the sex. That's what keeps it going. . . ." Fred told allmusic.com. "I took my pants off, and you were willing to let me sleep with you, and we did it—and you and I both wonder why we're not together. We don't respect each other or something; it was all physical."

Toning down the aggressive nature of their lyrics and music took on added significance in the wake of the shooting deaths of high school students at the hands of their peers at Columbine High School in Colorado. As people struggled to come to terms with the tragedy, wild fingers were pointed at musicians such as Marilyn Manson, who makes adults far removed from understanding his artistic approach, uncomfortable. Rather than blame the guns that were easily accessible to the students, some blamed the lyrics in songs for prompting the kids to violence. This kind of panicked atmosphere caused people in bands like Limp Bizkit to take stock of their own work and to try and decide if they felt they were negatively impacting America's youth. Wes called Fred after the tragedy and the two discussed the idea that their music might possibly be having this kind of affect. "I was like, 'Dude, no way,'" Fred said to the *Baltimore Sun*. "We don't have any lyrics that you could even put in that category. God forbid in heaven that anyone—anyone—listens to this record and thinks that it's in any way an invitation for them to do something violent, like hurt another human being."

# Five

When it came time to put the tracks on wax, Limp Bizkit decided to work at NRG Studios in Los Angeles and picked producer Terry Date to sit behind the boards. Known for his work with Pantera and White Zombie and more recently with the Deftones and Limp Bizkit protégés Staind, Wes told *Guitar One* that Date got the nod because of his laissez-faire production style. "He's just a wizard at sound. We chose Terry because he doesn't actually do what a 'producer' does—he doesn't get overly involved at the 'music' end of things. He's a producer who fools with sound and sonically makes everything perfect. He gets sounds that translate really well on tape and pretty much completely captures what we do, perfectly."

At the outset, Fred told MTV that Limp Bizkit believed it to be the ideal time to begin recording, since "Faith" was peaking and curious listeners were eager to hear what would come next. "We have to do this for our real fans who have been there since the beginning, you know. They've been listening to the same album for a long time and everyone else just now checking Limp Bizkit and listening to 'Faith.' [We] know it's all new to them, but our old fans have been having the same old record, so we got to give them something new."

Interscope wanted Limp Bizkit to rest up after Family Values and take a well-earned break. Under the label's timetable, *Significant Other* would come out in the fourth quarter of 1999, meaning sometime between October and December. Drummer John Otto told the *Rock N Roll Reporter* web site that the band nixed the label's plan because they were playing so well together at the time. "We came straight off the Family Values tour right into the studio. Most bands, before they get ready to do the second album want to kick back and take a break. But we were ready after touring because we were fresh and tight. It makes total sense to us because our chops are tight. Recording like that is better for us and we got it all thrown down onto tape by Christmas."

Limp Bizkit set the bar high going into the studio. Rather than adopt the "Aw shucks, we got a couple songs that are maybe ok" favored by some of the more timid rock stars, Fred went 180 degrees in the other direction in predicting what kind of record Limp Bizkit would make. In an interview with the *Alternative Press*, Fred said the first songs written for the record compared favorably to tunes by more established acts on albums widely considered to be among the decade's best. "We've got four softer songs; three or four in the 'Stuck' vein with phat hip-hop verses—crazy ambient hip-hop. But I think when we finish this, it's gonna be like the first Korn record or the first Rage Against the Machine record—one of those records that's just like the fuckin' bomb."

Danny Wimmer, owner of the former Milk Bar and friend of the band visited Limp Bizkit during the recording of *Significant Other* at NRG just as he did while *Three Dollar Bill Y'all* was becoming a matter of public record at Indigo Ranch. Wimmer said the two studios could not have been more different from each other. "NRG is a totally modern amazing facility. It's totally the opposite of Indigo. Indigo is so classically done, to me one didn't have anything on the other. Here [NRG] it's so nice and the technical part of it is so great. . . . This album was totally like Limp Bizkit structured everything. Terry Date brought all kinds of good tones. He's an amazing engineer in my book. Ross [Robinson] is more of a structure guy who will break down songs and add more to them. Terry Date is more of an engineer on the new album and it's the band that really produced this album."

Echoing Wimmer in an interview with the Rock N Roll Reporter web site, John said Date had an intuitive understanding of their music that made working with him easy. "He really captured our vibe very clearly. He's also really patient. We're one of those bands that's one big musical brain. We produce ourselves and Terry gets it on tape. He knows how to take how you want to sound and record it that way. He's really an amazing engineer."

The all-star cast assembled by Limp Bizkit during the recording of *Significant Other* varied from Method Man, who the band met while playing the MTV New Year's bash, to Durst's pal Scott Weiland, who in addition to offering Fred some singing tips, became a regular in the studio. Fred, in particular, eagerly pursued Method Man for the album, having long loved his unparalleled flow and off-kilter rhymes as part of Staten Island's rap collective Wu-Tang Clan. "I met him [on] New Year's. He had heard about us and he liked us. I told him I wanted to work with him, and he said that would be awesome because he hadn't done anything with a rock band yet," said Fred to allmusic.com about the origin of "N 2 Gether Now." "We held him to it, and he came through. We just sat down in the studio together and wrote rhymes."

With Method Man signed on Limp Bizkit realized that hinting at hip-hop with Lethal's smooth accents wouldn't be enough. In honor of having Meth, a.k.a. Hott Nickelz, a.k.a. Johnny Blaze, a.k.a. Johnny Dangerous, as part of the project, Limp Bizkit went the whole hog and wrote an actual hip-hop track. Constructed from some musical musings by DJ Lethal, Wes said Limp Bizkit made a point of approaching the tune from the hip-hop side of life. "Lee had been programming and making a lot of beats and a lot of hip-hop stuff, and he and Fred had wanted to get down and do some nitty-gritty MC/DJ stuff to really get into our hip-hop roots," said Wes to *Guitar One*. "So we wanted a track that was straight hip-hop."

Afterward Fred expressed similar sentiments to *MTV News* and suggested that getting too cutesy with the song might have actually alienated fans. "I think if Method Man came on our album to jam, they wouldn't want us to do some crazy-rocky-eclectic-artsy song to see what Meth and Limp could create that's crazy. What people want to hear is that 'I came to bring the pain' thing . . . and 'They call me Big John Stud/My middle name Mud.' I mean, that's what you want to hear, and that's what you got."

What fans got, in addition to Method Man's guest spot was DJ Premier of Gang Starr, producing "N 2 Gether." One of hip-hop's top producers, with production credits that include KRS-One, Jay-Z, Nas, Rakim, and the Notorious B.I.G., DJ Premier's involvement with the project in terms of cred was to producing what Method Man is to rapping.

Originally tagged "Shut The Fuck Up," for the chorus line that runs through it, Sam said the milder title of "N 2 Gether Now" was selected with an eye toward keeping the track marketable in the Wal-Marts and Kmarts of the conservative retail world. "I guess they just didn't want that because you can't really go too far with that publicly," Sam said to hiponline.com. "Having Method Man on it is like groundbreaking. Method Man doesn't do shit for anybody, especially a bunch of white boys. [laughs] We wanted to be able to put it out publicly."

Sam said the eventual collaboration between Limp Bizkit, singer Jonathan Davis of Korn, and Weiland on "Nobody Like You" came about coincidentally during one of Weiland's frequent visits to NRG studios. "He really dug the stuff that we were doing and he stayed around and helped out. He listened to the record and gave us hinters and ended up doing a song with us," said Rivers in an interview with hiponline.com. "The Scott Weiland and Jonathan [Davis, lead singer from Korn] thing was a spur of the moment thing. Jonathan happened to walk in and Scott Weiland was already there so it was like, 'Let's do a song.' A lot of it wasn't even planned."

Fred credited Weiland and his experience fronting the Stone Temple Pilots, with enhancing his own singing style. "He's a friend through friends of mine. He's a genius musically and he's got great ideas," said Fred to the Addicted To Noise web site. "He helps me sing right. There's proper ways to use your body to sing, to use your diaphragm and things. You want to expand. You want to take what you can do to the next level." In an interview with *MTV News*, Fred said Weiland saved him from another kind of vocal coach that apparently runs rampant through the music industry. "His musical sense is great you know. . . . The best singers in the world, whether you like them or not, have had vocal coaches and I'd rather have one that's someone that I really loved and bought his records myself instead of some fat little gay guy."

Echoing Fred's enthusiasm, Wes told *Guitar One* that Limp Bizkit was almost in awe of their larger-than-life guests while they were recording. "Well, we've worked with Jon, obviously, a lot before and have been touring with him for so long, so he's a dear friend. But Scott Weiland was another 'Method Man'-type of figure. Having a 'monster of rap' and a 'monster of rock'—two people that we look up to—on our record was amazing. Our mouths opened when they were in the studio."

Fresh off a stint in the studio with Limp Bizkit, Weiland gushed to *MTV News* that bands like Limp Bizkit and friends were helping to revitalize what had become a stagnant rock environment. "There's starting to be some excitement within rock and roll again," Weiland said a couple months before he was jailed on a drug charge. "You know, I think rock and roll and alternative music has gotten fairly stale and kind of boring in the last couple of years, since the earlier part of the 90s. And there's some good things happening again, sort of like a breath of fresh air. You know, bands like Limp Bizkit and Korn . . . Orgy, and a few others."

One musician who didn't appear on the record but who nonetheless had an influence on the recording of *Significant Other* was Lisa Gerard, of Dead Can Dance fame. Wes told *Guitar One* the melody from one of her solo songs came to him while on a bathroom break, and sparked the idea for the Middle-Eastern tone of the guitars on "Nobody Like You." "So I went to pee, and I actually was humming one of Lisa Gerard's melodies . . . and then kinda started thinking of other melodies— making up melodies in my head, but with her voice singing them—and I was like, 'Wow. I bet if I did that with real fast picking, like a balalaika or whatever the Russian instrument is . . .' That's what I was kinda shooting for, that kind of sound mixed with a Middle-Eastern flavor."

With the Internet helping to shrink the distance between the audience and performers, fans of Limp Bizkit were able to go online and learn about the new album from sporadic postings Wes made on Dike 99's Limp Bizkit web site. On the same day Wes first heard the rough mixes of *Significant Other*, he posted the following item about the new song, "Don't Go Off Wandering," signing his entry, "Tongue of Colicab," one of his many nicknames:

> I heard the strings on that song for the first time today and the melodies were so amazing. My brother Scott wrote the parts that the quartet played, on a keyboard and I heard that version of the song, but there is no substitute for the real thing (the actual cellos and violins) playing the parts. What else can I say without giving too much away? I will just say this, I am so proud of this record.

Even with Fred's passion for perfectionism, Wes cited the importance of staying open-minded to the unexpected accidents that can crop up during the recording of an album, that can help further the creative process and take the song to new and unanticipated places. "Mistakes and faults are good. They'll add that texture to a record," said Wes in an interview with *New Music Monthly*. "Sometimes a mistake will become important to the point where you go back and change everything else, instead of fixing the mistake."

As fans, the members of Limp Bizkit spent hours studying the albums of their favorite bands, like Jane's Addiction and Tool with every note, flaw, and tone taking on added meaning with each listen, and as a band they turned the same meticulous approach to monitoring the progression of their new album. Far from the decadent image fans tend to have of a rock band recording a record, Limp Bizkit's descriptions of their time in NRG make molecular biology seem like something you might do for fun. "We are all completely anal about every fucking note of music," said John to CMJ's *New Music Monthly*. In the same interview before the release of *Significant Other*, Fred detailed the depths of his anxieties. "Our record's not even out yet and I can think of ten ways to fix every song. We should just push the release back a month, I'll go back in and do this and this . . . I'm a pain in the ass for everybody who works for me, without a doubt."

John's quest for perfect beats on the record pushed him to seek out new drum tones and to consult with drum techs for advice on getting just the right sounds from the skins. "My drumming hasn't developed technically, but it has in the sense that I know how to pace myself now," John told the Rock N Roll Reporter web site. "This time, we spent a lot of time on the sonics of this record. If you listen to our albums back-to-back, sonically the new one is much more broad. For me, the drum sounds are really killer. I had a different drum kit and I spent a lot of time on tones with the people who built my drums."

As professed opponents of soloing, guitar or otherwise, it came as a surprise to John when Fred asked him to put together an extended drum solo in the middle of "Nobody Like You." Over a looped bit of tape assembled by Wes and Sam, John got a chance to show off his chops in true classic rock style. Having only played drum solos in the comfort of his own bedroom, he had some doubts but ultimately wound up with a percussive piece he could live with. "I don't think drum solos are totally appropriate for our band, but I think that because we've never done it, it was totally appropriate . . ." John told *Drum!* "I started going for it and had them rewind and take it back to the point until I felt comfortable with what I was doing . . . It's not the most perfect drum solo, but there are just certain things that are going on there."

Scott Borland, Wes's brother, played keyboards on "Just Like This," "Nookie," "Re-arranged," "I'm Broke," "9 Teen 90 Nine," and "Lesson Learned," reprising his role as the band's invisible sixth member. Making it a family affair, Fred's mom Anita stepped into the vocal booth and offered her matronly two cents for the "My Billy Goat," interlude asking Fred if he remembers a song from his childhood. And while not a blood relative, Staind singer and Limp Bizkit protégé Aaron Lewis got worked into the mix as well. Lewis confided to *9mm* that his vocals on "No Sex" might be mistaken for keyboards but were in fact a low-budget bit of studio trickery. "I sing all the backup vocals and that bridge section at the end. All the vocals that are on that song that isn't Fred is me. One of those little interludes there that sounds like a keyboard isn't a keyboard, it's me singing through a rubber piece of hose."

Seeking to stretch themselves musically, Limp Bizkit added two violins and a cello to "Don't Go Off Wandering," which Wes told *Guitar* One were intended to give the song an added emotional dimension. "My brother wrote keyboard parts based off the guitar parts that I had been playing, and then the string arrangers came in, took his keyboard parts and my guitar parts and did kind of a mixture of them. I think we were thinking a lot more 'classical'; we wanted a really emotional, dramatic piece of music."

In addition to his backing vocals and vocal coaching, Weiland also acted as Limp Bizkit's bullshit detector, at the band's behest, advising the band on which songs would be the bomb and which songs were duds. "Fred wanted an amazing singer to be an 'outside ear,' to listen to everything. We brought him in, and we were like, 'Well, what do you think of this?'" Wes informed *Guitar One*. "'Cause we're all really self-conscious, and we're our own worst critics. We'll get to the point where we hate everything—where we're like, 'None of this is good enough!'"

One song that Limp Bizkit decided wasn't good enough was one that probably could have been a hit just for its list of credits. But the tentatively titled

"Turn Me Loose," that featured Fred and Eminem rapping over a snippet stolen from the Madness song "Our House," never quite clicked and missed the cut for *Significant Other*. In an interview with the web site Addicted To Noise, Fred outlined the premise of the song. "It's about me and him walking into a party together, and he's chillin' out and getting faded, meeting chicks, and he's telling me he's on MTV and telling me his record's coming out. But then I come around and all the chicks wanna hang out with me 'cause I sold more records, stuff like that. It's pretty funny."

Still, despite the entertainment value and the luster of the star quality, Fred told *Guitar* that Limp Bizkit left the tune off the record because they felt it didn't quite gel the way they thought it should. "We were kind of forcing it to happen. Most of the keepers happened because we didn't force them. . . . The vocals were all there. Me and Eminem laid our vocals down, back and forth, and it was so good. But music-wise, we didn't nail it. And we're not going to put out something where it's like, 'Oh, wow! Eminem and Fred from Limp Bizkit? This is a novelty song.' "

Limp Bizkit's decision to pass on a ready-for-radio hit carried added weight given Eminem's reluctance to make guest spots at the drop of a hat. "The trend right now in hip-hop is to get every dope rapper you can and get 'em on your album," Eminem told the *L.A. Times*. "But I'm not really a collaboration-type MC unless it's somebody that I'm extremely cool with. If I see somebody that I like and respect, then I'm gonna get down with them. It has nothing to do with what type of music it is."

Having kept in touch with Primus singer/bassist Les Claypool since touring with him a couple years earlier, Limp Bizkit invited Claypool to record an introduction for the album. What began as an intro became a nearly three-minute spoken word piece. "I came in and they wanted me to write some sort of intro for the record. I got stoned and got in front of the mike and started babbling and they ended up not using the intro and using that instead."

As if their ubiquitous presence on MTV didn't fully drive the point home, Limp Bizkit got a tacit endorsement from MTV VJ and rock arbiter Matt Pinfield who agreed to pontificate on how refreshing Limp Bizkit's music is in an age full of radio caca in a recorded rant for the album.

While less overtly angry than *Three Dollar Bill Y'all*, lyrically Fred's angst remained close to the skin on songs like "Re-arranged," where he sings about the frustrations inherent in achieving great success in his career with no girlfriend to share in it with him. "It's about not having any support," he told *Rolling Stone*. "I'm a workaholic, and I need approval and reassurance. My brain never stops—it's a serious problem. I think myself to sleep, and

I wake up before my management, calling the office until they answer the phone. I gotta know everything. I have nothing to my life but work—I need to step back and smell the roses. Because I think the roses are starting to bloom."

Or in the more straightforward terms Fred used in describing the lyrical differences between the two records to CMJ's *New Music Monthly*. "The first record was about anger, instant reactions to my feelings. On this record, I'm accepting everything. Bad things don't stop happening when you get famous. But instead of just going, 'You did this to me? Fuck you,' now sentiment's more like, 'You're doing this to me? Ok. I'll accept that you did that . . . and here's the result.' "

Sparing no modesty, Fred bragged about the vague power of the title of *Significant Other* for Limp Bizkit's second record, in an interview with MTV. The open-ended title can be interpreted in a variety of ways, which Durst trumpeted as being the beauty of the thing. "*Significant Other*. It's like, such a title, you know what I mean?" Durst began. "There's no limits to what it means. Anything it was before—record, band, attitudes, feelings—it's the significant other. This is . . . the new level. Whether it's a lower level or a higher level, we'll let our fans determine that."

By the time famed producer and engineer Brendan O'Brien began mixing *Significant Other* at Southern Tracks Recording in Atlanta, Georgia,

Limp Bizkit was confident they'd succeeded in making the record they set out to make. Drummer John Otto declared to the Rock N Roll Reporter web site that Limp Bizkit's latest was head and shoulders better than their earlier effort. "It blows our other record straight out of the box. We went insane because that sophomore curse is a bitch. We went crazy and then wrote a bunch of the stuff and put it down on tape. We geared a lot of this material towards the things that have worked for us live. We got a lot more mature about writing and just refined some stuff. That's where we are right now."

With the album bagged and tagged and ready for the man in the store, the only thing left to do was to turn the masters over to the label, and to sit back and wait and see if *Significant Other* would sink or swim.

Bouyed by the success of the "Faith" video, Fred decided to take the reins for the "Nookie" clip and further establish himself in another field. Setting up outside, Limp Bizkit tried to capture the energetic vibe of their frenetic stage show just outside of Manhattan in Long Island City, Queens. With the first thousand fans on hand welcome to take part in the festivities, Fred took his cues from U2's "Where The Streets Have No Name" video. Fred explained his vision for the clip to MTV. "Just invite them all down to play in the raw, pirate style, like full-on U2 'The Streets Have No Name.' I love that video and what they did. I want to do the same thing for a different time, something for our fans of today to get."

Playing live meant that the fans moshing around the outdoor stage and the hired dancers in their matching khakis had to stay as dedicated as the band and maintain their energy and accuracy throughout the numerous takes. Fred choreographed the dances and dictated which shots were used but he downplayed his video know-how in an interview with MTV. "The fans bring the energy. We vibe off them. I mean, we did the song thirty times today and you can't do that without the energy there. They bring that element to the music. They are the reason it happens. You don't really have to know how to work the camera or have knowledge of the technology, you just have to surround yourself with the right people and know what you want to see."

In an interview with hiponline.com, bassist Sam Rivers described the electric atmosphere when Limp Bizkit took the stage for the filming of "Nookie"—kids were swarming the set trying to be one of the moshing many that made it into the clip. "There was a huge line. They had all the kids waiting on the sidewalk and it sounded like a roller coaster. We were in the alleyway and every once in a while you could just hear this roar of kids. And we were like, 'Damn! How many kids are out there?' It was killer."

At the conclusion of filming, Fred had good things to say about his work, telling MTV that the scenes in the clip are what rock and roll are all about. "The fans, the girls, live shows, you know, I would say everything but alcohol's in this video, which is you know, you don't need alcohol to have a phat rock show. Throw in the Limp Bizkettes to do a little girl power dancing, and there you go, you have yourself a little fat ass video in an alley."

As the release of *Significant Other* neared, Limp Bizkit became a staple of MTV's *Total Request Live* video countdown and the band themselves surfaced with a regularity that must have made album guest speaker and MTV's ex-VJ/resident bald guy, Matt Pinfield, jealous. "You don't realize how much a little bit of MTV'll do for a new, different band," Durst pointed out in the July 1998 issue of *Alternative Press*. With appearances on *TRL* and a New Year's gig in New York with MTV, Limp Bizkit got a big bit of MTV, a move that helped spike up their already brisk record sales. Among those glued to the tube in the middle of the day for the *TRL* countdown were Fred's parents, Bill and Anita Durst. In a few short years, the 'rents had graduated from watching their son rock the Milk Bar, to watching Fred and his band battle it out with Kid Rock for the number one requested video in the country. In an interview with the *Florida Times-Union* Bill Durst still sounded dazzled by it all. "It makes you almost burst because you're so proud," Bill says. "But then again it's so surreal. You sit back and wonder what in the heck is going on. . . . It's totally fascinating to me that here's a group of kids that probably never made more than ten thousand dollars a year and then they get together and make a hundred times that in a few short years."

# Six

In the spring and summer of 1999, Interscope geared up for the release of *Significant Other*, and seeing Limp Bizkit on the cover of a magazine became about as much of a novelty as seeing sand at the beach. The band, or band members, appeared front and center on the front of *Spin, Smug, Request, New Music Monthly, Guitar, Guitar One*, and were featured on online sites such as Addicted To Noise and Wall of Sound. Fred and friends failed to land their mugs on the cover of *Rolling Stone* but still were the subject of a several page feature and received the lead review when their album came out. Heady stuff for a band that only a year earlier had to shell out a pretty penny to get a Portland radio station to play "Counterfeit." Limp Bizkit's arrival as a solid box office draw and a megaselling act afforded the band the opportunity to thumb their collective noses at the multitude of critics who slagged them on their way up.

Even before the release of *Significant Other,* Fred noted the irony inherent in rubbing elbows with industry insiders that a year ago wouldn't have given them the time of day. "It's cool what's happening to us. We've done a lot of groundwork, toured a lot, dealt with a lot of shit—a lot of people telling us they couldn't stand us," Fred told the web site Addicted To Noise in February of 1999. "And those same people are praising us now, and that's pretty funny. But I guess that's what it's all about in the music industry. The only things that are real are the bands and the fans. . . ."

Some other real things are money and fame— and after the success of "Faith" Fred and friends had plenty of both. "I've finally got money in the bank, and I'm getting more free stuff than I've ever gotten in my life," Fred said to *Spin.* "It's so good to be a rock star, dude. People notice you wherever you go, you get into clubs, and you get into restaurants dressed like crap when you're supposed to have a suit on."

The perks that come with fame are obvious and plentiful and it's not hard to see what made a wanna-be baller like Fred swap the folksy feel of Jacksonville, Florida for the bright glare of Hollywood's spotlight. "This kinda shit I get off on. I'm at parties with Jack Nicholson, Dana Carvey. I'm at places where they hang out—I'm on all the A-lists. You get rock-star parking," Fred *told Rolling Stone.*

Being at the A-list parties also means partying with the A-list hotties. In the summer of '99, Fred's name was linked with Carmen Electra, Jennifer Rovero, a *Playboy* centerfold from Jacksonville, and an unnamed MTV exec who according to an article in *Rolling Stone,* got brushed aside when Carmen came to town. Carmen won the approval of Mom Durst, for one, who got to meet Ms. Electra at the Limp Bizkit show in Jacksonville in the summer of 1999. "We spent the whole time backstage with her, and she's such a sweet girl," Anita told the *Florida Times-Union.* "She was just precious . . ."

One of the invites Limp Bizkit snagged as their star brightened on the dark horizon was an invite to George Lucas's Skywalker Ranch in Marin County for a sneak preview of the much anticipated new *Star Wars* flick, Episode 1: *The Phantom Menace.* There, along with fellow newbie rockers 98 Degrees, Third Eye Blind, and a horde of movie and TV stars, they got a preview of the film and a tour of Lucas's house. Which MTV just happened to get on tape.

In spite of the preponderance of evidence that suggests Fred spent the months after the release of *Significant Other* cultivating a long list of new insignificant others, in interviews he made a point of claiming to be celibate. "That's not my scene," Fred declared to allmusic.com. "If you're really into that, then that's fine. But it's not what I'm into. Being a rock star, I'm in a position where I could be sleeping with a lot of girls and taking advantage of a lot of chicks. But I'm not sleeping with anybody. There are so many beautiful girls out there, but if you just want a girl because she's beautiful . . . That might be cool, I guess, if that's what you want." However, after that particular interview Fred backed off his celibacy-stance somewhat in a chat on twec.com. "Unfortunately I have broken that statement since the interview, but I am trying to keep the nookie to a minimum."

Still waiting for the love of his life to walk on in, the only permanent occupant of his Hollywood home, is an English bulldog named, appropriately enough, Bizkit. In an interview with the *NME*, Fred extolled the virtues of the canine kind. "Everybody should have a puppy because it's just so amazing how much you can love an animal. You can love everything about it, even the bad stuff, but another human being, you couldn't do that. I just think dogs are the shit, man. People who don't have dogs are weird."

Basking in the spotlight comes as natural to Fred as sliding his red Yankees cap on backward each day, but not all of his bandmates enjoy soaking up the attention the way he does. Having been mobbed plenty while out and about with Fred, and before with the House of Pain, DJ Lethal has worked out an airtight plan to avoid overzealous fans. "Man, I love Fred to death, but I hate going to malls with him. All the kids recognize him immediately, and what we wanted to buy in ten minutes becomes what we didn't want to do for an hour," Lethal told *Smug* magazine. "When Fred starts to sign autographs, I duck into the crowd, pull my hat down low, and ask him for an autograph, too. That way I get off the hook in no time. I'll tell you what, the day I can't run errands in peace . . . I'll quit this shit." Fred's mom Anita, spoke simply of similar trips with Fred to Jacksonville's Regency Mall, sadly remarking to the *Florida Times-Union*, "He can't even go to Applebee's anymore."

Cashing in on rock-star status and seeking the freedom to eat at Applebee's probably played the biggest role in Fred's move to California. However, in some interviews Fred expresses the concerns that come with the flip side of fame and the backlash of success. In an interview with allmusic.com, Fred seemed stung by the number of his former friends that turned on him. "I don't have any friends there, hardly. Most of my friends have all talked shit or betrayed me. The ones that haven't, I guess, are my true friends—those are the ones I need. But there aren't a whole lot of those. It's really hard to determine who are your real friends these days, with all this stuff happening. But I guess you know that the ones who betray you are not your friends."

Even as he's become as recognizable as Mickey

Mouse, Fred told *Rolling Stone*, there are still times that he feels his success to be a hollow triumph without a significant other to enjoy it with. "I play up the pimp thing on purpose. Like, when I'm on MTV, these chicks are fanning and massaging me. It's not like I attracted 'em off the street. We fucking hired 'em. I want everybody to be thinking I'm having the time of my life, but I'm single and miserable. I'm lonely. I'm experiencing the best things in my life, with no one there to share them."

Fred as the-lonely-rock-star-on-top-of-the-world became a recurring theme as Limp Bizkit played everything from the MTV studios in Times Square to sold-out arenas to late-night talk shows. Even with all the fame and attention, the story remained the same. Fred was just a lonely Southern man looking for the one. "I have so much fun doing what I do. I love being a rock star. I love making music. I love being on TV. I love making people get inspired by something that I create," said Fred to allmusic.com. "But just a small part of my life is the emotional side—like, I have a little domestic kind of vibe. I'd like to be with my soulmate. I'd share everything. But these other interviews make me look so pitiful and so lonely. I'm not like that."

As a leader of a band that prides itself on its efforts to keep it real, Fred is painfully conscious of how his move from Jacksonville can be perceived. Yet his desire to fully exploit the possibility fame offers, made Hollywood the only logical spot on the globe for him to set up camp. "I'm sure everyone in Jacksonville hates me for moving here. But I can't be back there without thinking about all the shit I went through," Fred lamented to *Spin* magazine. "And there's just more I can do here. In L.A., I can be at dinner and happen to run into a director or producer. That could lead to another album or a movie or someone wanting me to do a sponsorship with Calvin Klein clothes."

From a band standpoint having Fred on the left coast could have been construed as a problem, and at the very least would seem to make practicing with any kind of regularity difficult, but Wes told the web site Wall of Sound that Fred's move to Beverly Hills has had little impact on Limp Bizkit. "[DJ Lethal] was on the other coast, too, for a while, and it gives us a break from each other. John and Sam and I don't even see each other, and we're on the same coast. When we have a break, everyone takes off and does their own thing; that way when we come back, it's all new and fresh and we bring a lot of new stuff to the plate."

Fred's move west came less than a year after he proclaimed in the pages of *Spin* magazine that he had no intention of leaving his southern headquarters in Jacksonville. "I'm never going to move to New York or L.A. I'm going to stay here in redneck-ass Jacksonville and hang out with my redneck friends at my redneck cookouts." Although Fred Durst is hardly the first to be enticed by the gleam of Hollywood's twinkling lights, his move from the relaxed environs of Jacksonville to the hyperactive haven of Hollywood only makes sense in the context of Fred's long-term goals. Fred outlined the full extent of his vision for *Rolling Stone*. "I want to be the only musician who puts true, good, original thoughts into music and into films that have a major impact worldwide. I want to do it on a huge level. I can nail it in both worlds, really do it, man. That's where I'm heading: I wanna be Freddie Ford Coppola."

Adding bodyguards might also be construed as a rock-star move but in discussing his newly hired heavies with allmusic.com, Fred sounds much more like a banker than a rocker with an entourage.

"People start fights with me. Now that we're in this position, you can't really get in a fight or you'll be Axl Rose jumping into a crowd and getting sued. People will want to fight you now just to get money. If you hit them, even if they started it, they could get money off you. . . . People wonder why we walk around with bodyguards and security. It's for those exact reasons."

Protecting himself from overexcited fans is easily solved by hiring some no-necks as bodyguards but finding a way to deflect critics sharp arrows is not as simply done. In the same *Spin* profile that talked about the new Limp Bizkit record, the writer went on to say that Limp Bizkit had yet to write a good song. In an interview with *Smug*, Fred talked about what it's like to be the target of such finely pointed darts. "We just got majorly stabbed in the back by *Spin*. Not only [were we] misquoted, they added words in. That's fucked up, man. We want to sit down with the tapes and sue their fucking asses. The guy fully said the album's shit and [we] have yet to write a good song. I didn't realize they were the magazine that rips everybody."

Not all of Limp Bizkit's critics were of the ninety-eight-pound-geek music journalist variety, shock-rocker Marilyn Manson took a swipe at Limp Bizkit as well. He challenged the idea that Fred grew up as an outcast and derided their music in a blistering screed on his web site, calling them, "The kind of illiterate apes that beat your ass in high school for being a 'fag' now sell you tuneless testosterone anthems of misogyny and pretend to be outsiders to a world that they were born to wear their ADIDASS-FILGERING uniforms in. And we buy it up, helplessly."

Fred dismissed the sniping from Manson as sour grapes from an artist whose last record sold less than expected, and he took a jab at Trent Reznor of Nine Inch Nails while he was at it. In an interview with the *NME* Fred said, "I understand that Marilyn Manson is very unhappy that his career has gone in a shambles and he's alienated his fans, so if he has to say things like that because he's very mad at himself, I would forgive him. And Trent Reznor's in the fucking same boat. Trent Reznor is obviously unhappy with how he's alienated the world, how long he took to make a record, and how he thought he was immortal."

The inevitable backlash also included fans, angry at seeing Limp Bizkit become regulars on MTV. Feeling like the band they had followed from the early days wasn't theirs anymore, pious young fans entered chat rooms and trashed Limp Bizkit for selling out. Both Wes and Fred spend time online and read what the fans have to say. Responding to the OG Limp Bizkit fans on Dike 99's web page, Wes offered an explanation on how things work in the music industry for fans who are young enough not to be worried about little things like paying bills.

"Do you really think that MTV is a bad thing? I'll tell you what, if it weren't for MTV there would eventually be no Limp Bizkit, because we would all be broke and poor and have to quit because the music business doesn't work like you think it works. We are not rich. Every song we have ever written has been from the heart. We do not write what we do not feel and bro, you need to get over 'Faith.' That was a fucking joke that we never intended to blow up. But I am sure glad it did."

With no multimedia vision to chase and no groupies to have celibate fun with, Wes juggles his rock-star duties with some decidedly more domestic concerns, like finding some stolen seconds to call his wife while on tour. In an interview with *Smug*, Wes explained how he and his wife handle the time apart while he's on the road. "It's really hard at first to find balance between a family and being in a totally on-fire rock band and living like an insane nomad. Somehow we're doing it. She lives her life, I live my life. But when we're together, we have a great time. We're good friends and that's why it works."

Fred summed up the differences between his world and the planet of the apes that Wes lives on, in an interview with allmusic.com. "He's engulfed into his relationship and other things. There are just some people who want to stay home and be left alone and deal with little things in their little world. Maybe being out on the road when he goes on tour, that's enough for him creatively, and he's creative where he is. My vibe and surroundings, I need to be where opportunity is around each corner. . . ."

# Seven

In the weeks before the release of *Significant Other,* a steady buzz began to float and hum around the Interscope offices as publicists and presidents began to think that the new record Limp Bizkit had cooked up was stuffed with all the right ingredients to reach the top of the charts. Wes described Limp Bizkit's attitude in the weeks before the album's release and their reaction as it shot up the charts in an interview with launch.com. "Everybody had been telling us that was probably going to happen, but we didn't believe it, and we didn't want to jinx it. But it was really insane, the whole [first] week and the whole wait for it. There were people at Interscope talking about pooling money and making bets and stuff. . . . Everybody in the band's totally freaked out and giddy with excitement. . . . small town guys from Jacksonville, Florida, take over the world—at least for a couple weeks."

Even as the execs at Interscope were getting ready to watch sales of the new record sail into the stratosphere, Fred wondered if the band had succeeded in making an album that fans would latch onto. Wracked with self-doubt, Fred battled the idea that the band might have peaked and fans would give it a listen and head straight back to Tower Records to trade it in for somebody else's record. "I'm scared that they just won't get it," Fred told allmusic.com. "It doesn't sound like the first record. I'm not screaming at the top of my lungs every second of this record. But I'm worried that people are gonna be disappointed and they're gonna take it to a used CD warehouse. But I'm my own worst critic. I beat myself up about everything."

Wes said the whole band, not just Fred, had doubts before the release. "We just put this record together and hoped it would be accepted by our fans," said Wes in an interview with launch.com. "I wasn't thinking about a No. 1 on *Billboard*; I was thinking, 'God, I hope all the Limp Bizkit fans all like this.' That was about it. Everything else was an added bonus for me. We didn't feel like it was coming together until it came together. It was really like that, like we second-guessed ourselves up to the last minute."

Although they all had their doubts, Fred's insecurities were balanced with outbursts of confidence, such as the one that poured out of him in the same fretful interview with allmusic.com. "Everything seemed natural. It seemed like Limp Bizkit has evolved, and we really meshed it fine and smooth. It's like going from a Hanes T-shirt that's comfortable to a Calvin Klein T-shirt where the stitching is a little bit more professional, and the cotton they choose is a little bit softer and better. It's like Tool going from Opiate to Undertow, or Nirvana going from Bleach to Nevermind—that kind of a jump in maturity."

Jim Kerr, alternative rock editor for the trade magazine *Radio & Records*, said industry anticipation for *Significant Other* became palpable after "Nookie" was released to radio and station program directors began to get a sense of what a radio-friendly unit shifter they had on their hands. "On the radio side I think by the time the album was going to the stores there was a tangible feeling that this band was going to be huge. The requests for 'Faith' were through the roof and as 'Nookie' came out, they were even stronger even ahead of the album's street date. Based on airplay they knew it was for real, the question was 'How big was it going to be?' and that was answered after the first week of sales. I think it didn't surprise people who believed in the band and people who didn't believe turned into believers."

Among the converted was Fred's dad Bill, who told the *Florida Times-Union* that while *Three Dollar Bill Y'all* didn't really get his party started, the slicker style of *Significant Other* was right up his fifty-something alley. "We're kind of reliving our childhood through him. We were all from the Woodstock generation, and we're just reliving it through different music . . . getting used to the music takes a little time. The first album they did [*Three Dollar Bill, Y'all*] I really didn't care for. There were two songs I liked. But now that we're into this kind of music, and we listen to it more, I've found on the second album that there are only two songs I don't like."

Riding the momentum fueled by "Nookie" Limp Bizkit turned to a hit-and-run concert campaign to drum up even more adolescent excitement about the new record. On June 13, 1999 the Bizkit boys stepped onto the roof of a parking garage located at 121 Brookline Avenue, which is within spitting distance of Fenway Park, where Boston's beloved and beleaguered Red Sox gamely battle the Curse of the Bambino each year. Plugged into a generator, Limp Bizkit played a twenty-five-minute set to 1,500 hastily assembled fans that crammed the area after the location was leaked on WBCN. Rock historians will note that the Beatles thought to lug their instruments up the stairs and plug in high above the city of London nearly three decades earlier, but Limp Bizkit's Peter Katsis said the rooftop gigs were not so much an effort to teach the old rock dog a new trick, but instead served as a reminder of what a cool trick it can be. "There are no new gags in rock 'n' roll. It's how you bring back the old gags," Katsis told the *Boston Globe*. "The band loves this city. It was the first major market to give them airplay—and the band wanted to give something back."

The *Boston Globe* reported that the band left only after the cops came to interrupt the fun and games. Fred explained the band's sudden exit thusly: "We've got to get out of here or we're going to be arrested." Undaunted Limp Bizkit went on to play "secret" (wink, wink, nod, nod) shows in Detroit on June 15 and Chicago on June 16 to larger crowds each time, before facing the furious heat of the fun police.

In addition to generating a flurry of free publicity, Fred told the *Boston Globe* that Limp Bizkit's string of secret shows was all part of keeping things in the all important realm of real. "This is guerrilla style. This is set up and play until you get shut down. We're just fans who got lucky and sold some records," said Durst. "We've got to let people know that we're just like them—we're just fans."

Mike Peer, music director of WXRK, New York's K-Rock, told *Billboard* online, that his station's request lines were being flooded with calls for "Nookie," before the release of the album and that part of the excitement stemmed from the sudden viability of Adidas-rock. "Limp Bizkit is more than a rock band. They're part of a lifestyle movement going on which is similar to the grunge-rock movement of the early 90s. It's a movement of rock bands

with rap in their music: artists like Korn, Limp Bizkit, and Kid Rock. The fans are extremely passion-
ate about this music. We're constantly getting calls
to play 'Nookie,' and the anticipation for this album
is tremendous."

With froth-mouthed Limp Bizkit fans counting
down the seconds, minutes, hours until the album's
release, the only question remaining was how high
up the charts would they go. The Backstreet Boys'
tight grip on the top slot had lasted five weeks and
young ears seemed to be more in tune with the
synth sounds of their choreographed pop than anything involving that archaic instrument, the guitar.
So Limp Bizkit was holding their collective breath
before the album's June 22 release. The announce-
ment that the band had rocketed to No. 1 on the
*Billboard* 200 albums chart came as a much-needed
exhale of relief. Limp Bizkit shot past both the
Backstreet Boys and Ricky Martin on their way to
the top of the heap, with *Significant Other* selling a
staggering 643,874 copies in the first week of release, according to sales-tracker SoundScan. Lest
anyone attempt to write off their ascendancy to
pop's throne as a fluke, Limp Bizkit rebounded the
second week with a robust 335,000 records sold according to SoundScan and with nearly one million
records sold in two weeks, reigned supreme.

Staind guitarist Mike Mushok was on tour with
Limp Bizkit when word came that those who bet

on *Significant Other* going No. 1 in the office pools had just gotten richer. In a posting on Staind's official web site Mushok described the debauchery that followed. "Thirty-eight people piled into one of Limp Bizkit's buses and we went down to Sixth Street and proceded to take over one bar after the other. It was pretty crazy. I don't think the night ended for most people until like eight the next morning. It was a rough next day!"

The necessary carousing completed, John Otto took a moment to reflect on Limp Bizkit's triumph in an interview with the Rock N Roll Reporter web site, admitting that when the five of them were trying to con their friends and their friends' friends to come see them at the Milk Bar, he never could have predicted Limp Bizkit would go No. 1. "I didn't think this would happen. You can't plan for it, but you hope something happens. I look back and we've done a substantial amount of work in a short amount of time. Our goals are straight and we want to keep writing phat music."

Limp Bizkit's timing with the release of *Significant Other* was nothing short of impeccable. Lewis Largent, vice-president of music at MTV, told the *Miami Herald* that the newest generation of the record-buying public has been thoroughly indoctrinated into the school of hip-hop and their ears couldn't be better atuned to listen for crossover acts. "You're finally seeing this new generation of people, and to them, rap is what rock was before," Largent said. "That's why you're hearing hip-hop in Korn and Limp Bizkit and Kid Rock."

In an interview with Wall of Sound, Wes described Limp Bizkit's music as a natural evolution and acknowledged that their arrival on the scene was right on time. "It's obviously the next progression, as far as high-energy music. It was the mix that was coming. . . . A lot of the same vibe is in both hip-hop and rock. The hip-hop world has looked to guitar for influence as well, like Public Enemy and a lot of the bands that were sampling guitar and Led Zeppelin, and a lot of the beats are John Bonham playing drums."

Jim Kerr said the stellar sales of *Significant Other* are indicative of Limp Bizkit successfully making the jump from hungry road warriors to established heavyweights. "Look at the sales numbers. The question was, 'Is there demand for Limp Bizkit?' Apparently there is, but measuring demand isn't a one week thing. You have to look at the following weeks and see how much it tails off. By staying on top they showed that this is not a band that's being driven by a small number of core fans. This is a mass appeal band that has entered the mainstream of young America. This is what young America is listening to."

And young America like the hip-hop. At the same time *Significant Other* topped the charts, Kid Rock was making the transition from journeyman musician to bona fide rock star and on the other side of the ball Puff Daddy's dabbling with rock enlisted the aid of classic rock giants Jimmy Page and Sting. In an interview with the *Miami Herald*, Puff Daddy talked about how he brings his rock influence to his rap music. "I'm a big fan of all that—Kid Rock, Godsmack, Limp Bizkit. I love their raw energy, their aggression. I have an alter ego on this album called P Diddy, my rock alter ego. It ain't no gimmick or nothing. It's just another side to me from when I was growing up, listening to rock."

With record sales quickly topping the million mark, it was time for Limp Bizkit to deliver the live goods. Beyond being a way to reach new fans, over the years performing live had become a cathartic experience for the band, a phenomenon Fred explained in an interview with the *Boston Globe*. "It's something to see people with a vibe and glow in their eyes. Everybody is there for different reasons and that creates one gigantic ball of energy that hits you in different ways. Certain people are singing certain lyrics, and some girls are screaming, and some other people are crying and feeling other stuff. It's so many different emotions. It's the most powerful thing in the world. I've never experienced anything like that. It's like an adrenaline rush takes over."

As part of readying for the tour, John and Lethal

once again had to make sure they were on the same page as each other, needing to interact particularly carefully on "No Sex." In an interview with *Drum!*, John talked about the adjustments necessary to nail "No Sex" live. "The beginning of the song, I have to be pretty much on the right exact tempo, because the sample's in time. [Or] I have to start a little bit up to the sample. Because if I play the beginning too fast when the chorus hits, that whole sample is just worthless."

Seemingly, the first few weeks after seeing *Significant Other* rocket to number one should have been some of the best days for the band, but Limp Bizkit's summer tour schedule yielded some rocky times with a significant injury, an arrest, and a major stain on the band's image. For starters, on June 22, the opening night of Limp Bizkit's Limptropolis tour with fellow pimp rocker Kid Rock, the injury occurred. Frustrated by the sound at Seattle's Mercer Arena, bassist Sam Rivers smashed his bass to bits, cutting his hand in the process. The gash stopped the set and took ten stitches to close. After a pregnant pause Rivers returned to help Limp Bizkit give the crowd "Nookie" and finish the set. Staind were the openers on the tour and guitarist Mike Mushok described the scene in a posting on Staind's official web site. "He had to go to the hospital for a few stitches but he returned within the hour to finish the show. It was awesome. The ambulance pulled up doing like sixty mph and he jumped out and went to the stage to finish the set. It was great—nobody left."

Taking band frustrations out on unsuspecting equipment is not an unusual occurrence for Limp Bizkit. In an interview with the *Baltimore Sun*, Wes acknowledged that when things take a turn for the worse, Limp Bizkit's instruments tend to pay the price. "If we're having a good show, we don't break anything. You hit a certain point, and you just become violent. Not necessarily toward people. But if we're having a bad show, stuff starts getting demolished."

Sam's return to the show post-hospital made headlines nationwide and reinforced Limp Bizkit's image as a band committed to putting on a good live show, even if it takes a couple hours and some stitches to get it done. However, after a flurry of screaming ink touting the ascension of *Significant Other* to first place, the next set of headlines screamed something else entirely. Fred's arrest on assault charges stemming from the July 12 incident when he allegedly kicked a security guard in the head during a performance at the Roy Wilkins Memorial Auditorium in St. Paul, Minnesota, cast a bit of a pall over the band's success. Part of the uproar revolved around Fred's reaction. On the stage Fred seemed unrepentant regarding his alleged actions. "I kicked that punk-ass security guard in the head," Durst said according to St. Paul police. "That fucking bitch, you ain't gonna get a check tonight.

Where's that fucking security guard? Where is that fucking pussy bitch?" The victim, Pat Estes, received treatment for blurred vision and equilibrium difficulty at United Hospital in St. Paul.

In an interview with allmusic.com Fred discussed his more volatile side. "I have a temper, but it comes out in spurts. Sometimes it doesn't come out and sometimes it does. What people don't understand is, I'm not like that all the time. If you're an asshole, there are some times when you're not. I'm a human being. I'm very unpredictable. My behavior is very unpredictable, and my mood swings are very up-and-down."

The incident in St. Paul made Fred's temper a matter of public record, but in an interview with *Request*, Wes said the rest of the band is quite familiar with Fred's sudden outbursts and have gotten used to working around him. "Fred will sometimes totally explode and try to knock the monitor guys over the head with a microphone stand, or he'll attack people onstage. Sometimes he'll walk off after just one song or he'll break every microphone at a huge show on purpose and just not sing. You never know when he's gonna totally lose it, but it's better than working with someone who's totally predictable."

In July of 1999, one could not argue with Limp Bizkit's commercial success. The kids bought millions of their records, MTV put their videos into heavy rotation, and even Fred's parents were watching *Total Request Live* to see if the Jacksonville five managed to beat out Kid Rock each day. About the only segment of the population that didn't make at least some clumsy attempt at leaping onboard the Bizkit bandwagon were the critics. *Spin* openly clowned Limp Bizkit in a profile and *Rolling Stone* took a smug tone in writing about the band. The *New York Times* took a similar stance in Ann Powers's review of Limp Bizkit's July 22 show at the Hammerstein Ballroom. Powers derided Fred's outsider stance and said he couldn't sing. "DJ Lethal used his turntables as a metal guitar, riffing expansively and going for effects instead of rhythm. John Otto on drums and Sam Rivers on bass never even tried to get funky, instead steering hip-hop's breakbeat-based structure into a backbone for power chords. This makes for a hybrid that would be more interesting if the band did not constantly mire itself in boring tempos, and if Mr. Durst had any talent as a singer." Undaunted, Limp Bizkit headed north to Rome, N.Y. for a gig at Woodstock '99, a show that Limp Bizkit would be criticized for in a manner that would make Ms. Powers's thoughts about them as a band seem kind.

Getting picked to play Woodstock is a band's dream. Drummer John Otto told the Rock N Roll Reporter web site that he thought their selection might be the thing that would finally get people to know Limp Bizkit for being Limp Bizkit, and not Korn's little buddies. "It's so amazing that I'm tripping out, man. Our music speaks for itself now. We're past the point of being compared to other bands. When a band first comes out, people love to compare them to someone else to see if they're copying a style. If you think we sound like so and so, you have some serious issues happening."

With a star-studded lineup that included Korn, Rage Against the Machine, Red Hot Chili Peppers, Alanis Morissette, Metallica, Jewel, Elvis Costello, Kid Rock, Willie Nelson, Bush, and James Brown to name a few, the weekend of July 23–25 was meant to be the concert event of the year. It was, only not for the reasons promoters might have hoped. The recent reincarnations of the legendary hippie-fest may not be the cultural phenomenon the first one was, but they have gotten more hype than almost any other shows in recent memory.

The 1999 edition was not so much mud and free love, but more of a reenactment of one of Fred's favorite flicks, *Apocalypse Now*. Ending in a fiery riot that caused Flea of the Red Hot Chili Peppers to make the comparision to the legendary film, the beginning and the middle of the festival were reported as a waking nightmare filled with angry dehydrated fans and alleged sexual assaults. Press coverage of Woodstock pointed a finger at the more aggressive acts on the bill, with several publications pointing the finger directly at Limp Bizkit, for inciting an already riled-up crowd.

The controversy swirled around Fred's onstage

comments. "People are getting hurt. Don't let anybody get hurt. But I don't think you should mellow out. That's what Alanis Morissette had you motherfuckers do. If someone falls pick 'em up. We already let the negative energy out. Now we wanna let out the positive energy," he had said. And although Limp Bizkit had left the festival by the time the fiery riots began to burn, most of the complaints centered around the brutal activity in the pit during their set. As the media tried to make sense of 1999's three most infamous days in rock, allegations surfaced that a young woman was sexually assaulted during Limp Bizkit's aggressive show, where Fred crowd-surfed on a piece of plywood over the audience's outstretched hands. John shared his recollections of the volatile atmosphere at Woodstock in an interview with *Drum!* "We started a song and then stopped because Fred was going, 'Hey can you all hear me? And nobody could. Well people started to get pissed. Then they turned it back on. Just total chaos broke out, MTV people were running for their lives, Much Music people were running for their lives. . . . It was totally cool."

Not all media outlets criticized Limp Bizkit for adding to an already tense situation, but nonetheless the wave of reports that washed over the public had a decidedly negative undertow. "I didn't see anybody getting hurt. You don't see that. When you're looking out on a sea of people and the stage is twenty feet in the air and you're performing, and you're feeling your music, how do they expect us to see something bad going on," Fred later said to the *Washington Post*. "Woodstock was about makin' some money, and gettin' it in the quickest, easiest way they could get it on and down and done. A lot of people were hurt. A lot of people were scarred for life. A lot of people experienced panic in situations and things going on because of them."

Although Fred didn't see anybody get hurt, CNN described the carnage during Limp Bizkit's set thusly: "Things had turned ugly in the mosh pit Saturday night while Limp Bizkit was playing. More than two hundred people threw bottles, smashed a barricade, and nearly trampled sound-system components. One woman suffered a serious head cut from a thrown bottle."

Les Claypool of Primus dismissed the firestorm of negative press surrounding Fred's comments from the Woodstock stage as being a symptom of his love of the limelight. "You know, Woodstock was just Durst being Durst," Claypool told the San Francisco Examiner. "His attitude is no press is bad press, so he brings it on himself. He wallows in it. Still, he's a great guy."

Stunned at the ferocity of the negative attention, Limp Bizkit silently fumed about their media treatment at Woodstock, waiting and letting the video for "Re-arranged" express their feelings about the concert that ended in burning and looting. "It is about being persecuted for something you're not guilty of," said Fred to MTV. "No matter how hard anybody tries to get rid of Limp Bizkit, which everyone is trying to, we're gonna live forever. Whether we die, whether we go to heaven or whatever, the CD is there, it's not going anywhere. What we did at Woodstock was we went and did a Limp Bizkit show, and our shows are pretty intense."

The video begins with each of the five members in Limp Bizkit in separate cells playing their respective instruments, waiting to face sentencing for their role in the Woodstock chaos. After receiving a death sentence each member of Limp Bizkit defiantly continues playing the song, as milk pours into the room and angry-looking witnesses watch. Fred used the video as his artistic statement regarding what he and the band regarded as their role of scapegoat at Woodstock.

"They needed someone to point the finger at. They needed a scapegoat," Fred told the *Washington Post*. "They're not gonna put it on the dumb-ass who handed out candles to everybody and said, 'Let's capture a moment. I bet everybody's gonna light them and hold them up.' After these living conditions, after everything that happened, are they gonna do that or are they gonna burn it down? They're gonna burn it down."

In further defending his band to MTV, Fred suggested that the promoters were partially at fault for booking Limp Bizkit, given their reputation for delivering a raucous live show. "Our crowd, the maximum we've ever played for at a normal show is like twenty-five to thirty thousand. You multiply that times the three hundred thousand [that were there], you have to think like that, and no one thought like that. The living conditions were terrible, but I'm sorry. I didn't realize what was happening, but we're still gonna be Limp Bizkit and do what we do."

Even with, or perhaps because of, the flurry of bad press following Woodstock, *Significant Other* shot back to the top of the charts the next week. Confidence brimming, Fred boldly predicted to MTV that the 1999 edition of the Family Values tour would easily outdo the inaugural version headlined by band benefactors Korn, the previous year. "If you saw Family Values last year," Durst said, "[then] this year is times ten. This is bigger, phatter. It's just amazing, and I think that every year is gonna keep getting better. And I think we're gonna have guest appearances from people from last year. It's just an amazing thing for rock and hip-hop in this world and 1999 today."

Limp Bizkit's problems at Woodstock failed to impact their ability to secure dates for the Family Values tour. Gary Bongiovanni, editor of the touring-industry magazine *Pollstar* told the Addicted To Noise web site that concert promoters in all probability would view the incidents at Woodstock as an aberration and not hold it against the band. "No promoter [would refuse to] promote a

Limp Bizkit date at this point in time," he said. "The band's hot and they're selling tickets. The danger is if they develop a reputation where they might be considered a threat to public safety, and that really hasn't happened. People forgive an isolated incident. If it becomes a pattern, then people get concerned."

With rapper DMX a late scratch from the lineup, the Family Values clan included Filter, Method Man, Redman, Run-DMC, Primus, Staind, Ja Rule, Mobb Deep, and Crystal Method with Limp Bizkit esconced as the headliner. The tour began September 21 at the Pittsburgh Civic Center in Pennsylvania and ending Halloween at the Mississippi Coast Colosseum in Biloxi, Mississippi. As a surprise bonus, tour founders Korn joined Family Values in midswing, dropping in for a week's worth of shows, beginning October 5 in Grand Rapids, Michigan and sealing the deal with an October 13 gig in Minneapolis, Minnesota. A twenty-seven-date affair that ended up nearly doubling the gross of the previous outing, Family Values took in over ten million in receipts and on average played to approximately three thousand more fans each night than the previous year.

The improved numbers surprised Gary Bongiovanni, editor-in-chief of the concert trade publication *Pollstar*, and someone who pays close attention to these kinds of things. In an interview with the *L.A. Times*, Bongiovanni seemed to be at a loss for reasons to explain it. "It's actually something of a surprise. You'd think that Korn would have been such a huge headliner last year that they wouldn't be doing comparable numbers [this year], even though Limp Bizkit is hot at the moment . . . Maybe they did a good job of building the brand name its first year with Korn and the kids really enjoyed it, because I think a lot of the markets are repeats from last year."

The success of Family Values might have shocked industry insiders but from comments made by participants in the fall fling make it apparent why the Bizkit venture succeeded. Filter singer Richard Patrick told MTV the similarities between his act and Limp Bizkit helped make the fall tour a quality venture. "They're exactly like us, huge music fans. They love all types of different stuff, and my record goes from rock to acoustic, to very electronic, to kind of industrial, and back to rock again. I'm trying to break all these labels, because I don't want to fit into a genre. I want to be a hybrid of all of them, and that's the way Limp Bizkit is."

Les Claypool of Primus took the stage each night of their two-week stretch on Family Values in a blue crash helmet, stomping around the stage, leading his outfit through a mixture of older staples such as "Tommy the Cat" and newer tunes such as "Anti-Pop." "It went well," said Claypool of the tour. "We were only there for two weeks of it. It seemed like a pretty good scene. A lot of screaming teenagers. It was all good. I had a good time."

Members of last minute addition Mobb Deep couldn't say enough about Limp Bizkit in an interview with MTV. And Prodigy proclaimed, "I was blown away by the Limp Bizkit performance and the feedback that the crowd gave them." "Extraordinary," chimed in Havoc. "The show that they put out was ill," said Big Noyd. "That was incredible. It's like rap and rock are almost the same thing. But rock's just out there to more masses of people, and rap is taking it there," finished Prodigy.

Mike Mushok, of Family Values openers Staind, said in a posting on the band's official web site that his outfit was thrilled for the chance to play to the large audiences and thanked Limp Bizkit fans for taking a chance on them and coming out in time for their early set each night. "Well all I can say is that we're totally psyched to be on the first half of Family Values . . . YAE!! the shows have been going great! I want to thank everyone for showing up early and showing your support."

A veteran of earlier ventures such as Gathering of Tribes and Lollapalooza, Les Claypool said the Family Values tour's hip–hop-rock mixture seemed to mesh the best. "Obviously hip-hop has become extremely popular. We're festival whores. We've done them all. The first one was the Gathering of Tribes. That came along before Lollapalooza and never gained popularity. It was us, EPMD, Steve Earle, X, Fishbone, Johnny Law . . . and it didn't really take. It took the momentum of Jane's Addiction to get Lollapalooza going and it's only now that cross-genre touring is starting to get successful. When I was a kid, you were defined by the music you listened to and the car you drove, I would assume with these festivals being successful to an extent, that it's not a given. Things now aren't so clearly defined."

Including Method Man in the video for "N 2 Gether," was part of the shot of cred in the arm that Limp Bizkit got when the Wu-Tang warrior agreed to work with the band. In his best video to date, Fred played off the kung-fu imagery that Wu-Tang frequently raps about and manages to work in former VJ Pauly Shore. The beginnings of the "N 2 Gether" clip have their origins in the end of the video for "Re-arranged," when Fred says aloud, as he and Wes try to figure out if they're dead and in heaven, "Dude, if I were in heaven, I'd be kickin' it with Method Man right now."

The heaven that Durst envisions, surfaces as a world where he plays video games and spars with Method Man a la Kato and Clousseau and Pauly Shore delivers pizzas. "We have this really bizarre fight between each other that's [still] friendly," said Fred to MTV. "It's kind of like Peter Sellers and his butler [Kato] in *The Pink Panther*. Like we're fighting, and all of a sudden the phone rings and we stop . . . It's just a video that I think we needed to have and no one in a rock band with an amazing hip-hop artist such as Method Man has really crossed these lines."

Fred's appointment as Senior Vice-president of A&R at Interscope Records afforded him the opportunity to continue working with bands like Staind, who he helped get signed to Flip Records after they opened for Limp Bizkit. On October 23, 1997 Limp Bizkit played a gig at the Webster Theatre in Hartford, Connecticut. Staind guitarist Mike Mushok said in the band's bio, that his first encounter with Fred was a conflict. "Fred thought we were Satan worshippers due to the nature of our cover art. Of course we weren't, but they tried to have us kicked off the bill. Fred and I exchanged words. Then, he took our CD and threw it across the table; he wanted nothing to do with us—so much for our big break. Well, at least until Fred saw our show! After our set, Fred approached us and said we were the best band he had seen in two years."

Subsequent conversations led to Staind driving down to Florida and recording a demo with Durst, a session that Mushok said was instrumental in improving the vocals of Staind singer Aaron Lewis. "Fred played an integral part in helping us to develop our sound. Aaron, our singer, has an amazing voice and Fred helped to bring that out," said Mushok. "We had a lot of screaming parts in our songs. Fred said, 'Man, you can sing, why don't you do that more?' The trip was very productive because we reworked four of our songs and played a killer sold out show in their hometown of Jax."

Having helped Staind hone their sound, Fred took the next step in a move that recalls the way Korn helped kickstart Limp Bizkit's career. "While there, Fred contacted Jordan Schur, the president of Flip Records," explained Mushok. "Fred told Jordan about us and within a week of leaving Jacksonville, we were on a plane to L.A. where we met Jordan and recorded a three-song sampler." Wes discussed the similarities between Limp Bizkit's relationship to Korn and Staind's relationship to Limp Bizkit with *Maximum Guitar.* "Staind's demo tape blew us away. Fred brought them to Florida, let them stay at his house, brought in some DAT recorders and did a demo with them and sent it out. They played a showcase in L.A. at the Opium Den, and a bunch of major labels started drooling. Kind of like what Korn did for us in a way."

As a long-time friend of the band, former Milk Bar owner Danny Wimmer said reaching down to pull their friends up a rung on the ladder, has been Limp Bizkit's MO since they were nobodies in Jacksonville. "When they played with national acts, they always picked their friends' bands to open up for them. Once Fred's on your side, he's going to take care of you," Wimmer said, adding that he had once been offered Limp Bizkit's managerial slot. "He's going to try to get you to his level."

The career of Jacksonville standby Cold also got a kickstart from Fred. Having labored in obscurity for over a decade without a deal, the members of Cold were justifiably skeptical when Fred said he would bring them onboard, according to drummer Sam McCandless. Having somebody say, "I can hook you up" after a show generally pans out to be about as helpful as having fans tell a band how to better play their instruments, but this time the kid in the Kangol hat came through. "When he [Durst] told us we could get signed, it was like 'Yeah, right,'" McCandless said in an interview with the *Florida Times-Union*. "Then a couple of days later we got a call from him, saying that Ross Robinson [who produced Limp Bizkit's debut, *Three Dollar Bill Y'all*] had heard the tape and gotten goose bumps. He said that he wanted to record the album as soon as possible." In the summer of '97 Flip Records paid for Cold, then known as Grundig, to fly out to Los Angeles and record their record and then shopped it around to the majors, with A&M ultimately winning the bidding war and adding them to their roster.

Jordan Schur, the man who signed Limp Bizkit to Flip Records and their co-manager, helped broker the deal with Interscope—Flip's distributor—that made Fred a VP. "He has terrific vision, and he's very enterprising," said Schur to the web site Addicted To Noise. "He's worth any and all ambitions that he and the company have." Fred's interest in new bands comes at an intuitive level, he told the *Alternative Press* and no band that fails to pass a basic gut check, can catch his interest. "I want to be one of those people—someone who brings people in, breaks new bands . . . I can hear a new song and go, 'That's gonna be huge,' even if it's something I don't like. I go by cold chills—if I get chills on my arms, I know it's on."

Fred signing on as an A&R guy, follows the appointment of KRS-One as an exec at Reprise and perhaps could change the dismal state of the music industry, as described by Wes to *Maximum Guitar*, for the better. "There are so many people in charge of finding acts who have no taste in music whatsoever and are maybe a couple of IQ points from being retarded, and they have more power than God in the industry. And there are bands being signed by these people who are worthless wastes of money. Every band on the radio now I hate."

In a statement released by Interscope/Geffen/A&M, Fred acknowledged the opportunity his new position would provide but also pointed out that the title is meaningless if he doesn't put it to good use. "I'm proud to have this position, but it means nothing unless I take the title and put it into action. Interscope has already done amazing things to shock the world, and now I'm going to come in and create a musical revolution."

Fred's got his ducks in a row for life after Limp Bizkit but before he devotes his life to the cinema or spends all his days and nights in seedy bars looking for the next big thing, there is one thing he feels has eluded him and his Bizkit buddies. As he explained to *New Music Monthly*, he has goals that go beyond breeching the platinum barriers for sales. "I understand what timeless music, music that lasts forever, is. That's something Led Zeppelin tapped into, Elton John, the Doors. Jane's Addiction and the Cure and Nine Inch Nails made timeless music. Limp Bizkit hasn't gotten there yet, but we're a hell of a lot closer."

# Eight

Having established themselves as a force to be reckoned with, by notching a pair of multiplatinum LPs, the true test for Limp Bizkit is still a couple albums away. Bands with true staying power find ways to connect with audiences year after year and album after album, long after the first rush and flurry of fame has subsided. Once a few more records hit stores, history will be able to accurately judge if the Florida five are a flash in the pan or fit to rub elbows with veteran acts such as Lynyrd Skynyrd or the rock until you drop Rolling Stones that managed to shrug off the occasional overdose or accident and keep the band together. "You've got to keep going. Every day is different, and there's a million bands jumping in this world every day, and things change so quick, you gotta keep going with it," Fred said to the Addicted To Noise web site. "You gotta keep growing with your fans. The fans that liked us two years ago who were fourteen then are sixteen now; fans that were nineteen are now twenty-one—there's a lot of difference in thinking there."

Nikki Sixx, bassist of Mötley Crüe, spent much of the '80s selling millions of records and living the kind of life that VH1's *Behind the Music* episodes are made of. Overcoming addictions, arrests, convictions, and critics, Mötley Crüe kept their lineup intact until drummer Tommy Lee's departure in 1999, minus a one-album hiatus for singer Vince Neil. Although Sixx and friends set records for decadence that Limp Bizkit would be pressed to match, the bass player did pick up a couple tricks to sticking around. Sixx said one way to stay in the game, is to watch and learn from the survivors. "Always judge by the Rolling Stones. They've been here the longest. You always look to the oldest guy in the room. The Rolling Stones for our business are the template, and that's who we should all look up to," Sixx said. "They've been up and down a few times, especially during the '70s. Most bands when they get to that point, they usually break up because they didn't financially secure themselves and can't take it, and explode or implode. It's not about now and it's not about tomorrow. It's about the whole journey. That's where you stay doing what you do. Summer, winter. Summer, winter. It's going to be hot, it's going to be cold. It's like any other relationship, it takes work, it takes time. Success is the easy part. Longevity is the ticket."

Scott Ian, guitarist for the nearly two-decade-old Anthrax (their collaboration with Public Enemy on "Bring the Noise," sparked Wes to start listening to hip-hop) said Limp Bizkit should keep the pressure on their fans and challenge them with the next record, instead of trying to retrace their footsteps and make *Significant Other Part Deux*. "For a band like Limp Bizkit, at their level of success, the best thing they can do would be to come back and make a harder record. Maybe they won't get as much commercial success but what they'll do is solidify their street vibe. If they came out with a radio record after this, they would lose everything. The best thing to do is make the hardest record they could make after this, and fans will be like "Wow, they didn't sell out.' "

Max Cavalera fronted Sepultura from their formation in Belo Horizonte in 1984 until parting ways with the band in 1997. Max's ingredients for a recipe to keep the Bizkit hot and fresh runs along the same lines as Ian's, with a dash of determination, a smattering of innovation, and a whole lot of loyalty to the fan base that made their success possible. "You have to keep innovating and furthering yourself. Don't go backward. Don't turn your back on fans no matter what. They're the reason why you do the shit. They are your bread and butter. You can't dis the fans no matter how big you get. It's super important to be proud of your fans and have integrity with your fan base. That will probably do it. Look at people like Ozzy, he has three generations of a fan base. I see some young fans who have never heard of Sepultura and some that I recognize from the early days back in Brazil. The key is to have that common respect between you and the fans and always push the music forward."

One of the ingredients necessary for continued success is band chemistry, an intangible relationship between performers that goes beyond how well they all play their instruments. Les Claypool of Primus said in his time touring with Limp Bizkit and working in the studio on each others' records that this batch of Bizkit has got it in spades. "To be a good band or a good performer is purely a matter of taste. For a band to be a powerful unit, that's a different thing. It's the luck of the draw being able to get individuals that create that certain chemistry. It's a rare thing that doesn't come around all that often. A lot of times the units that do click aren't going to be popular. For the combination of the chemistry and popularity to be there it is a rare thing."

Kismet and chemistry have played a role in Limp Bizkit's getting a crack at the big time, a fact that Fred says helps drive his pursuit of other projects. In an interview with the *L.A. Times* Fred talked about wanting to capitalize on the tremendous opportunities suddenly tumbling into his lap. "We've been really blessed. You can be the most talented person in the world and be stuck forever in a place like Wichita, Kansas, if no one gives you a break. Someone put my foot in the door, and now I can get to use my vision."

Jim Kerr said the key to lasting in the music business can be as simple as finding ways not to self-destruct. "There's a couple things that play into an artist having longevity. One that they don't kill themselves and two that the band stays together, which I guess is related to my first point. A band will last if it doesn't implode and it doesn't seem like they are. They key to longevity is to keep writing great songs. If they keep writing great songs they can stop touring tomorrow, and stop doing radio interviews but if they keep putting out albums full of great songs, people will continue to love them."

Working on side projects that allow band members to pursue sounds that might not jive with the Limp Bizkit vibe is one way to keep members content. Fred's production credits include work with Primus, Staind, and he's popped up occasionally on albums by bands such as Soulfly, Korn, and Tommy Lee's Methods of Mayhem.

Les Claypool, bassist/vocalist with Primus credited Fred's production work with pointing their 1999 LP *Anti* in the more aggressive direction taken by their earlier records. Fred produced the anti-social glue-fiend anthem "Lacquer Head," which Les said got the band excited about resurrecting their former slap-happy skree. "Fred's a friend of mine. Those guys toured with us when they were coming up a couple years ago. Fred's a big Primus fan. I remember one night in particular we got drunk and were hanging out in his apartment and he said he wanted to produce our record and that it was the aggressive stuff that really inspired him. He really wanted to see us go back to that, slamming stuff out. It was kind of an awakening. He wanted to make it more of a balls out record and it wound up that we leaned more in that direction. He was like a cheerleader in the studio, trying to get us to play the aggressive stuff like we did in the old days."

Both Wes and Lethal have projects of their own in the works. Wes described the quirky musical force that is Big Dumb Face to the web site Wall of Sound. "It's kind of like Ween or Mr. Bungle, really silly and idiotic and bizarre. I've been doing that as a stress release for a long time, just making up stupid songs, some of it with my brother, some of it not. It's nothing but stupid; there's one song called 'Tit Adventure,' another called 'Mighty Penis Laser,' just all these retarded songs. If anybody buys it, it'll either attract, like, a really cult following, like Ween does or people will buy it 'cause it has something to with Limp Bizkit."

As for DJ Lethal's long-promised solo record, in an interview with *MTV*, Lethal intimated that the LP will be an all-star affair, with guest appearances from singers Jonathan Davis of Korn, Chino Moreno of the Deftones, Mark McGrath of Sugar Ray, guitarist Tom Morello from Rage Against the Machine, and of course Limp Bizkit's own Fred Durst. "I'm writing for it now, concocting some new potions!" said Lethal. "I'm gonna be recording it over the next few months on the road. I wanna do a rock song with just turntables." He adds, "There'll be a huge collaboration with a bunch of DJs. And for the rappers involved, I'm gonna have guitar stuff. For the singers I'll have more hip-hop stuff. All this will be interwined with mad keyboard/synth stuff, drum 'n' bass!"

Between his A & R duties at Interscope and touring and writing records with Limp Bizkit, it's not like Fred's hurting for things to do. If Limp Bizkit were to go belly-up, a career directing videos would not be out of the question. His work from the director's chair produced the MTV staple clips for "Faith," "Nookie," "Re-arranged," and "N 2 Gether." Sufficiently impressed Bizkit buddies Korn picked Durst to direct the video for "Falling Away from Me," opening doors for future ventures in the genre. Korn frontman Jonathan Davis credited Fred with providing a quality visual expansion of the ideas behind "Falling Away from Me," with his direction of the clip. "Fred came up with it, 'cause he directed the video and came up with the concept," Davis told MTV. "It was shot really well, and just stuff that kids go through, just showing it, and the whole thing of the video is to just see their salvation, basically. Our music is a release or salvation for kids to go to when they're feeling down. [The video] kind of portrays that."

The next step beyond video direction for Fred is film. Quite aware that no one is approaching the members of Warrant and Skid Row with film deals, Fred feels as though he needs to make hay while the sun shines. Fred explained his feeling of urgency to allmusic.com. "I don't want to have an amazing record, and do some killer things with my music, and then die out and say, 'Ok, trust me. I wrote this film. Believe in me. Because, remember, my band used to be hype and dope, so you can believe in me.' Right now my band is hype, and we're at another level, and I really have a vision for directing and writing movies and videos. Everything that I become involved with becomes successful. My hit-to-miss ratio is zero—all hits so far."

For about a year before any deal became official Fred made it known to a variety of sources that the flick he felt the world needed now was a hybrid of several TV shows and movies. Sometimes it was *Road Rules*, blended with *The Game* and *Breakfast Club* and in this particular interview with MTV, Fred saw it a little differently. "It's kinda like a, its probably an *Easy Rider* meets *The Breakfast Club* of 1999 with a really dark twist to it, a really real twist to it and Scott [Weiland] is going to be in the movie. He's going to have a really cool role in the movie, but I don't know if I should give away the character. No, because then I'd have to tell the story."

The long-discussed project got a name and a production deal in October of 1999, when Warner Bros. agreed to bring what had become known as *Nature's Cure*, to the big screen. TV writer Chris Kletzien wrote the script and filming was set to begin in early 2000, with Fred sitting easy in the director's chair. Fred's belief is that *Nature's Cure* will be the vehicle that drives him to become the only movie mogul with a backward hat and a flavor-saver. "It's something we've missed since the John Hughes days. It's gonna be amazing, and it's gonna let people know that there are artists out there that have a mad vision that can't be taught. I feel that God has blessed me, and that I'm really in tune right now. I see myself ultimately as a kind of Dr. Dre-meets-Steven Spielberg. That's me all the way," he said in an interview with *Request*.

While the side projects, the videos, and the movies all are on the agenda, the more immediate business of being the rock band Limp Bizkit still takes precedence. Drummer John Otto told the Rock N Roll Reporter web site that in the same way Limp Bizkit hustled back into the studio after touring for *Three Dollar Bill Y'all*, the plan to keep making records in a timely fashion is still a viable one. "We're actually planning on going into the studio to do another record soon. We're doing it because, back in the day bands used to pump out records left and right. There was no having two years in between albums. We're not just trying to pump out as many records as we can, because if it's not good, we won't release it. . . . We're always writing music and we even have Pro Tool recording gear in the back of our bus."

For now at least, Limp Bizkit remains as Fred's main course, with his other employment opportunities serving only as delectable appetizers. In an interview with the *NME*, Fred reasserted his commitment to the band that made the other options now at his disposal a possibility. "I've got my foot in the door but I'll never alienate Limp Bizkit, it's always first. I want both, I want it all. And if you deliver, you speak with actions and you don't expect something for nothing, you can have it all."

To Fred's bandmates, seeing Fred the mover and shaker get a vice-presidency at Interscope is still somewhat of a shocker. Wes told launch.com that the fact that the band finds it amusing won't stop them from capitalizing on it. "We just run around laughing about it, 'cause it's so ridiculous and over the top. We can't believe it. But we all are probably gonna put side projects out . . . because he's the boss. We'd be dumb not to use that opportunity, as ridiculous as it is."

Limp Bizkit is not necessarily everybody's choice to accompany their cup of tea. But as a band that gave themselves a name they wanted people to hate, keeping everybody happy hardly figures into the picture. As Fred said in an interview with allmusic.com, just before the release of *Significant Other*, Limp Bizkit will always have their detractors, but that won't be the thing that makes them close up shop. "The people who continue to slam us as being on some bandwagon are the people who don't care about growth. They don't care about reality, and they don't want to listen to it evolve. They just want us to be removed. And as long as those people keep writing shitty stuff about us, the more people become curious, and the more it's good for us."

In a business that's shifts and changes are made with no more notice than that given by a sudden gust of wind, a sense of perspective can be worth its weight in fool's gold. Wes, for one, seems to realize that the same forces that propelled Limp Bizkit to the top of the charts could very well be the same ones that cause them to drop somewhere below the radar into territory inhabited by the Vanilla Ices and MC Hammers of the world. In an interview with *Guitar*, the art student turned rock star offered his take on Limp Bizkit's chances for sticking around a while. "Being versatile is the main thing about being able to stay in the music and make a career out of it, because people are so fickle. They'll think one thing is awesome for a while, and then suddenly they don't like you anymore. I think musicians and bands should go with whatever makes them happy—just like Metallica. They're a lot older now, they don't want to play these crazy big riffs that blow people's heads off their necks."